ADB'S SUPPORT FOR THE SUSTAINABLE DEVELOPMENT GOALS

ENABLING THE 2030 AGENDA FOR SUSTAINABLE DEVELOPMENT THROUGH STRATEGY 2030

MARCH 2021

ASIAN DEVELOPMENT BANK

ADB

© 2021 Asian Development Bank
6 ADB Avenue, Mandaluyong City, 1550 Metro Manila, Philippines
Tel +63 2 8632 4444; Fax +63 2 8636 2444
www.adb.org

Some rights reserved. Published in 2021.

ISBN 978-92-9262-737-9 (print), 978-92-9262-738-6 (electronic); 978-92-9262-739-3 (ebook)
Publication Stock No. TCS210093-2
DOI: http://dx.doi.org/10.22617/TCS210093-2

Notes:
1.   In this publication, "$" refers to United States dollars.
2.   ADB recognizes "Korea" as the Republic of Korea and "Vietnam" as Viet Nam.

Cover design by Karmen Karamanian.

CONTENTS

Figures and Boxes

Figures

Boxes

Foreword

Rebuilding for the Sustainable Development Goals

President Masatsugu Asakawa

The vision of the Asian Development Bank (ADB) is an Asia and Pacific region that is prosperous, inclusive, resilient, and sustainable, reflecting the aspirations of the Sustainable Development Goals (SDGs).

The region was already off track to meet these ambitious goals before the coronavirus disease (COVID-19) pandemic began to wreak devastation around the world. The crisis triggered by the pandemic has laid bare fragilities in our economies and societies that can be linked back to failures to make sufficient progress on critical SDG targets. Hundreds of millions of people in the region are being pushed back into poverty, and the region's economic growth was negative for the first time in 60 years in 2020. Yet as countries seek to recover, we have a unique opportunity to refocus on the SDGs.

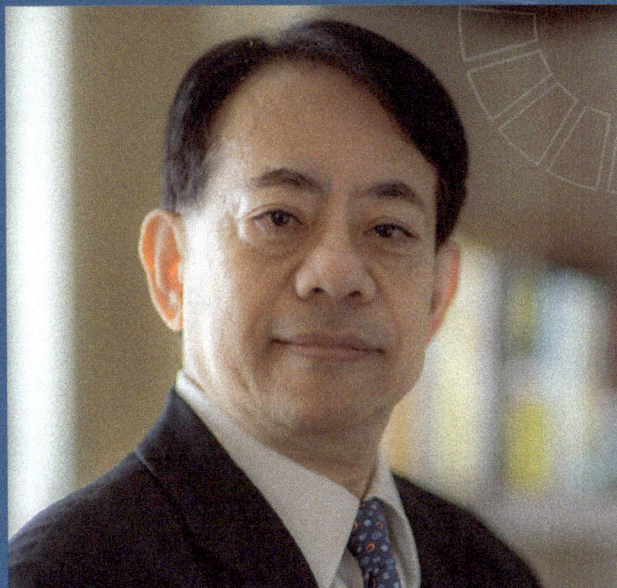

member countries can develop better tax policy and robust tax administration. Continued efforts to expand private sector investment that advances attainment of the SDGs with deeper and more fluid domestic and regional financial markets are also vital part of the financing agenda.

Managing the worst effects of COVID-19 on our societies was ADB's key priority in 2020. We launched a $20 billion

> **ADB's investments must meet the highest standards of sustainable development and deliver real results that help countries rebuild for the SDGs.**

This report explains ADB's support for the SDGs, outlining our approach to integrating the 17 goals and their associated targets throughout our strategies and policies, and highlighting the many ways in which ADB is helping countries make progress on this challenging agenda. The review provides a basis for reflection on opportunities to strengthen our efforts and sharpen our focus on SDG attainment through our operations and country engagement.

Achieving the SDGs will require vast sums of finance to be mobilized from the widest range of sources in support of the agenda at a time when governments face mounting pressure on their budgets and soaring public debt. Supporting countries to achieve SDG target 17.1 and strengthen their domestic resource mobilization is a key foundation for all other SDGs. ADB will further strengthen its support in this area through partnership with governments, businesses, and peer international organizations, so that our developing

package of support, followed by a $9 billion program to help our members access and deploy vaccines against the disease. In 2021, as we map a path to recovery from the pandemic, we must refocus on the SDGs. We must help countries navigate the difficult policy and financing choices that will aid the eradication of poverty, increase inclusion and tackle inequality, promote gender equality, and address environmental sustainability. Critically, in a year when countries must scale up their efforts in response to the climate change crisis if the Paris Agreement goals are to be met, we must ensure that recovery efforts support green and resilient development.

ADB's investments must meet the highest standards of sustainable development and deliver real results that help countries realize the vision set out in Strategy 2030 and rebuild for the SDGs.

Abbreviations

4Ps	–	Pantawid Pamilyang Pilipino Program
ADB	–	Asian Development Bank
ASEAN	–	Association of Southeast Asian Nations
ASEAN+3	–	10 ASEAN members plus Japan, the People's Republic of China, and the Republic of Korea
CAREC	–	Central Asia Regional Economic Cooperation
COVID-19	–	coronavirus disease
CPS	–	country partnership strategy
CRF	–	corporate results framework
DMC	–	developing member country
EMO	–	education management organization
ESCAP	–	Economic and Social Commission for Asia and the Pacific
FCAS	–	fragile and conflict-affected situations
GDP	–	gross domestic product
GHG	–	greenhouse gas
GRIS	–	green, resilient, inclusive, and sustainable
HLPF	–	High-Level Political Forum
Lao PDR	–	Lao People's Democratic Republic
MDB	–	multilateral development bank
NDC	–	Nationally Determined Contribution
OECD	–	Organisation for Economic Co-operation and Development
PKSF	–	Palli Karma Sahayak Foundation
PPP	–	public–private partnership
PRC	–	People's Republic of China
SDG	–	Sustainable Development Goal
SIDS	–	small island developing state
SMEs	–	small and medium-sized enterprises
UN	–	United Nations
UNDP	–	United Nations Development Programme
UNICEF	–	United Nations Children's Fund
YREB	–	Yangtze River Economic Belt

At home. Women in West Bengal, India rest by their houses after a day of chores (photo by Amit Verma).

Introduction

When the international community adopted the Sustainable Development Goals (SDGs) in 2015, they set out an ambitious new agenda for all countries to address the needs of people, planet, prosperity, and peace through strengthened partnerships and a shared focus on common development challenges. Count have taken significant steps to reflect the SDGs in their national development efforts. The Asian Development Bank (ADB) has been a committed partner in these efforts, supporting the engagement of developing member countries (DMCs) in the negotiation of the SDGs, aiding country implementation, and aligning its operations and results management systems with this global development framework.

This report showcases ADB's approach to the SDGs since they came into force in 2016, in the context of the implementation of Strategy 2030.[1] It complements the first joint multilateral development bank (MDB) report on the SDGs launched in December 2020 under the guidance of the Heads of MDBs.[2] Section I introduces ADB's approach to the SDGs. It reviews the region's progress and ADB's institutional strategy and articulates a theory of change for how ADB helps countries achieve the SDGs. Section II highlights ADB's efforts to support the SDGs. It reviews ADB's contributions to clusters of interconnected SDGs related to people, planet, prosperity, and sustainable infrastructure, as well as ADB's efforts to mobilize finance and knowledge in the context of SDG 17: Partnerships for the Goals. Section III concludes the report by highlighting opportunities to deepen ADB's approach.

---

[1] ADB. 2018. Strategy 2030: Achieving a Prosperous, Resilient, Inclusive, and Sustainable Asia and the Pacific.

[2] Islamic Development Bank and ADB. 2020. Financing the Sustainable Development Goals: The Contributions of the Multilateral Development Banks.

I. ADB'S Approach to the Sustainable Development Goals

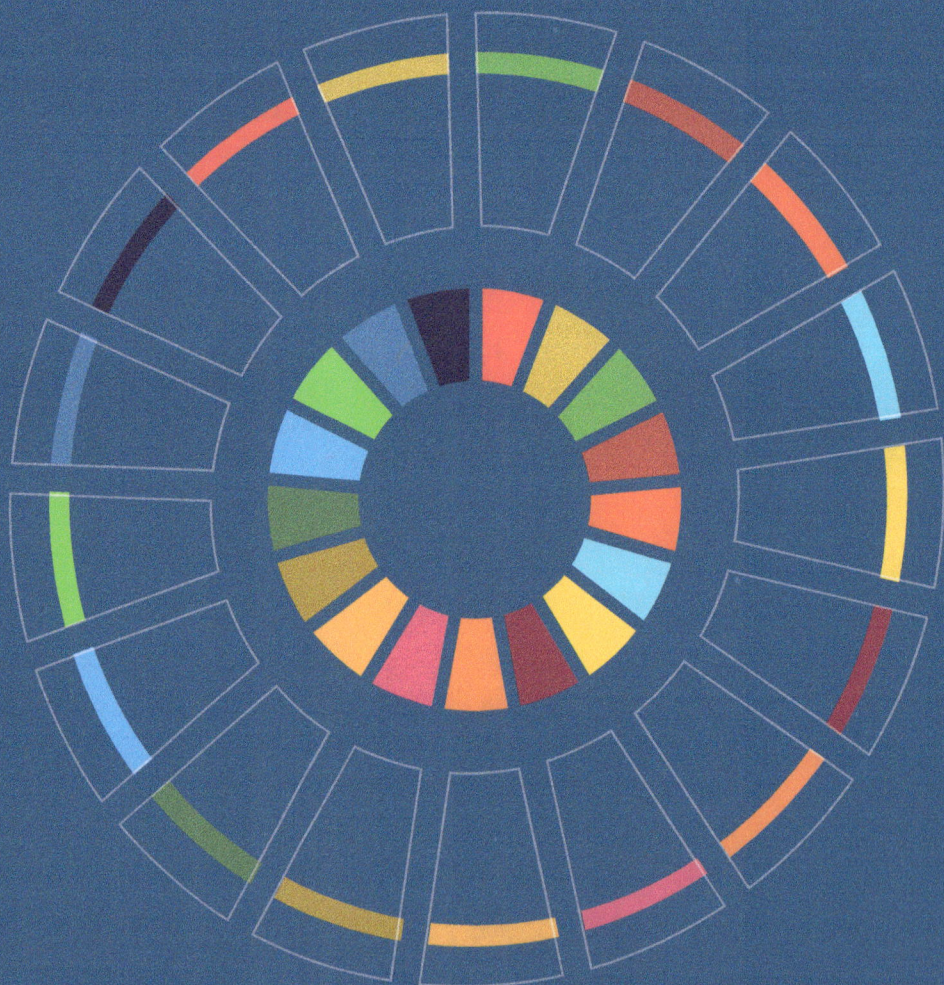

A. The Sustainable Development Goals in Asia and the Pacific: Progress and Implementation

ASIA AND THE PACIFIC

2/3 OF THE WORLD'S POPULATION

ROBUST ECONOMIC GROWTH RATE **+5%** IN RECENT DECADES

WHEN THE SDGS WERE ADOPTED IN 2015

273 MILLION LIVING ON LESS THAN **$1.90 PER DAY**

1.1 BILLION LIVING ON LESS THAN **$3.20 PER DAY**

ENVIRONMENTAL SUSTAINABILITY IS AN ENORMOUS CHALLENGE ACROSS THE REGION

The SDGs pick up where the Millennium Development Goals left off, providing a holistic and comprehensive integrated framework for development aspirations in Asia and the Pacific. Home to two-thirds of the world's population and some of the world's largest economies, the region maintained robust economic growth rates of more than 5% per year in recent decades. This growth helped lift billions of people out of extreme poverty, but when the SDGs were adopted in 2015, 264 million people in the region were still living on less than $1.90 a day and a further 1.1 billion were living very close to the poverty line on less than $3.20 per day, at high risk of being pushed back under it.[3] Progress has been diverse across countries. As wealth has increased, so have inequalities, and promoting more equitable growth that simultaneously advances SDG 1 (No Poverty) and SDG 10 (Reduced Inequalities) is a priority if the region is to truly leave no one behind. Issues of environmental sustainability, such as air and water pollution, climate change, inequality, and lack of resilience to natural hazards, are enormous challenges across the region. Analysis suggests that overall, countries in Asia and the Pacific have made more progress on the SDGs since 2015 than other global regions.[4] Nevertheless, ADB DMCs

were off track to achieve all 17 SDGs even before the coronavirus disease (COVID-19) pandemic triggered a sweeping human and economic crisis in 2020. The limited progress reflects in part the holistic and ambitious nature of the SDGs, a narrow focus on economic issues, and slow progress on several SDGs and their associated targets. Economic growth has not always translated into decent jobs for all. Progress in reducing extreme poverty left many people living very close to the poverty line, while inequality has been a pervasive challenge. There have been notable gains in providing basic services such as education, clean water, and energy. Environmental sustainability has been a particular problem, underlining the need for ambitious climate action, and more progress in increasing installed renewable energy and protecting life on land and below water amid extensive degradation of natural resources, including through more responsible consumption and sustainable production. Figure 1 summarizes ADB DMCs' collective progress on each SDG.

---

[3]   ADB. 2020. 2019 Development Effectiveness Review.
[4]   J. Sachs et al. 2020. The Sustainable Development Goals and COVID-19. Sustainable Development Report 2020.

Figure 1: Sustainable Development Goals Progress in ADB Developing Member Countries

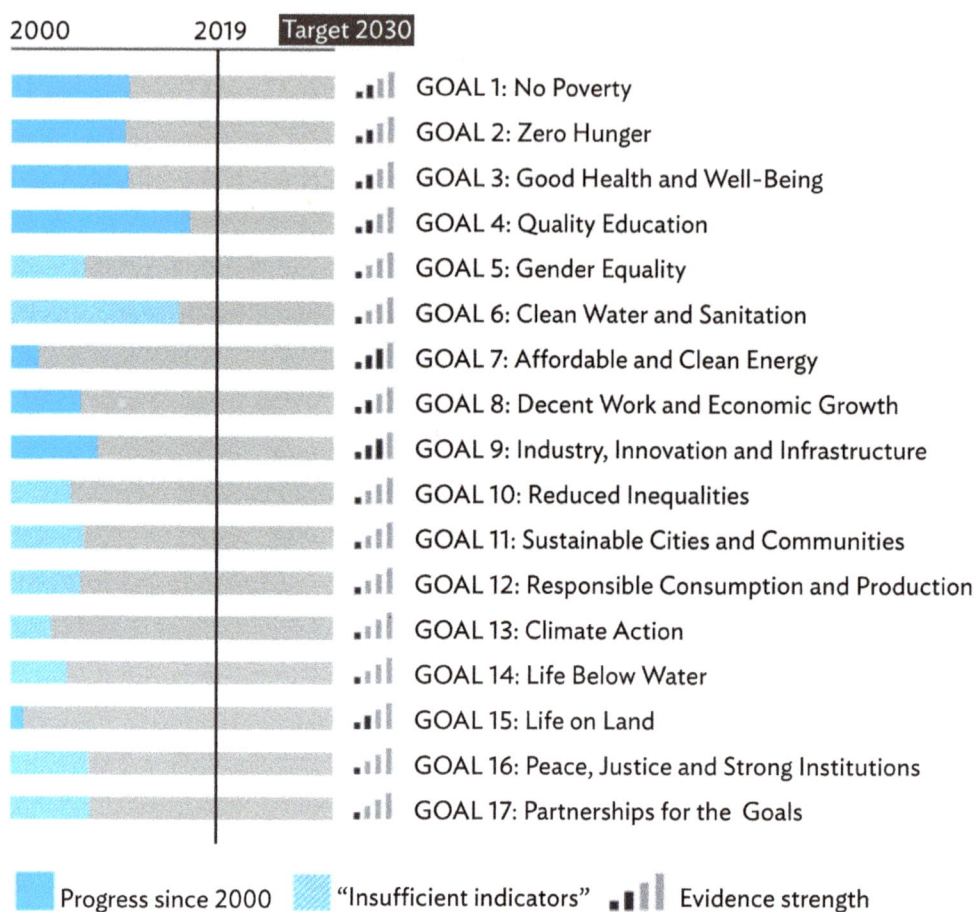

2000	2019	Target 2030		
			.ıll	GOAL 1: No Poverty
			.ıll	GOAL 2: Zero Hunger
			.ıll	GOAL 3: Good Health and Well-Being
			.ıll	GOAL 4: Quality Education
			.ıll	GOAL 5: Gender Equality
			.ıll	GOAL 6: Clean Water and Sanitation
			.ıll	GOAL 7: Affordable and Clean Energy
			.ıll	GOAL 8: Decent Work and Economic Growth
			.ıll	GOAL 9: Industry, Innovation and Infrastructure
			.ıll	GOAL 10: Reduced Inequalities
			.ıll	GOAL 11: Sustainable Cities and Communities
			.ıll	GOAL 12: Responsible Consumption and Production
			.ıll	GOAL 13: Climate Action
			.ıll	GOAL 14: Life Below Water
			.ıll	GOAL 15: Life on Land
			.ıll	GOAL 16: Peace, Justice and Strong Institutions
			.ıll	GOAL 17: Partnerships for the Goals

Progress since 2000   "Insufficient indicators"   .ıll Evidence strength

Note: The Economic and Social Commission for Asia and the Pacific estimates that data availability for the Sustainable Development Goals increased from 25% in 2017 to 42% in 2020. However, accurate data are still a lacking for many SDG indicators in many countries. In key, "Insufficient Indicators" indicates that there are too few indicators with sufficient data to ensure the robustness of the progress shown.

Source: Asia-Pacific SDG Partnership. 2020. SDG Progress.

1. Implementation of the Sustainable Development Goals in Asia and the Pacific

Countries in Asia and the Pacific engaged actively in the negotiation of the SDGs, and most have taken a range of measures to implement them. Globally, progress is reviewed through the High-Level Political Forum (HLPF) on Sustainable Development, where countries are invited to present voluntary national reviews of their progress in implementing the SDGs. By the end of 2020, 36 of 41 ADB DMCs had presented Voluntary National Reviews at the HLPF, 12 of them more than once (Figure 2).

The degree to which countries have prioritized the SDGs in their framing of national development challenges and engagement with development partners varies

significantly. Nevertheless, a range of measures have been taken and sustained to support national implementation of the SDGs. At least 16 DMCs have issued an SDG-related law or decree. Most DMCs have established institutional arrangements for SDG implementation. About 23 have established intragovernmental and/or multi-stakeholder mechanisms to support the agenda, while others are using existing mechanisms. Most countries have begun to align or integrate their national plans with the SDGs, and more than 30 have identified key points of convergence between their national development plans and SDG targets and indicators. Ten countries, including Bangladesh and Indonesia, have developed initial road maps or plans for SDG implementation, setting out national targets for the SDGs. Section II of this report includes "spotlights" that describe ADB's engagement with DMCs across the region on their SDG implementation efforts.[5] Figure 2 summarizes the measures DMCs have taken to implement the SDGs since 2015.

Several regional forums have been established through which countries can share and reflect on collective progress toward the SDGs and participate in coordination and collaboration opportunities. For example, the Asia-Pacific Forum on Sustainable Development convenes regional members once a year for this purpose, informed by subregional consultations on selected themes. Forums such as this can play an important role in revitalizing progress toward the SDGs in the aftermath of the COVID-19 crisis.

Figure 2: SDG Implementation in Asia and the Pacific

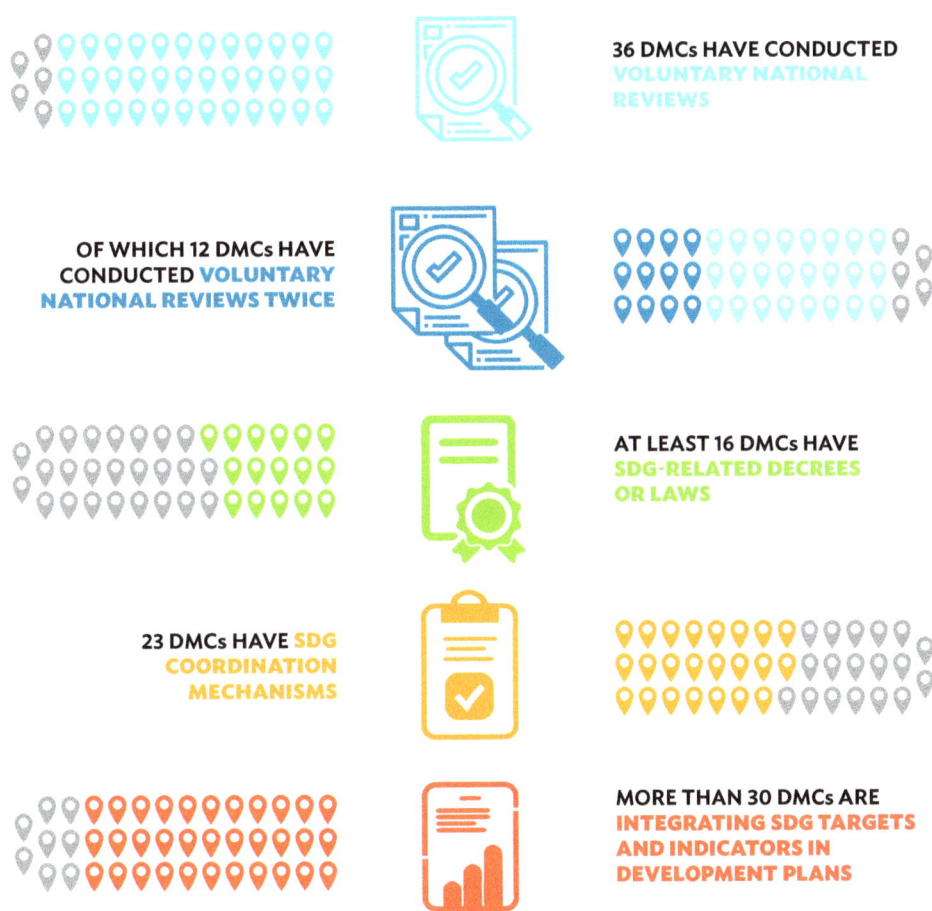

36 DMCs HAVE CONDUCTED VOLUNTARY NATIONAL REVIEWS

OF WHICH 12 DMCs HAVE CONDUCTED VOLUNTARY NATIONAL REVIEWS TWICE

AT LEAST 16 DMCs HAVE SDG-RELATED DECREES OR LAWS

23 DMCs HAVE SDG COORDINATION MECHANISMS

MORE THAN 30 DMCs ARE INTEGRATING SDG TARGETS AND INDICATORS IN DEVELOPMENT PLANS

= DMC

DMC = developing member country, SDG = Sustainable Development Goal.

5   The indicators are from the ESCAP–ADB–UNDP Asia-Pacific SDG Partnership data portal (Asia-Pacific SDG Partnership. SDG Progress).

Trying to get by. Nine-year-old Safeer sells masks in the streets during the COVID-19 lockdown in Pakistan (photo by Rahim Mirza).

2. Implications of the Coronavirus Disease Pandemic

The immediate impacts of the COVID-19 pandemic on macroeconomic stability, economic growth, human development, and environmental systems will have wide-ranging implications for all the SDGs. ADB estimates that the gross domestic product (GDP) of developing Asia and the Pacific contracted by 6.0%–9.5% in 2020 compared with pre-COVID-19 projections.[6] Global economic losses could reach $4.8 trillion–$7.4 trillion in 2020, with developing Asia accounting for $1.4 trillion–2.2 trillion, or about 28% (footnote 6). By the end of 2020, the crisis had already pushed 78 million more people below the $1.90-a-day poverty line.[7] In Pakistan, for example, the International Monetary Fund estimated that in June 2020 up to 40% of the population were living below the poverty line because of COVID-19, following a decades-long decline in poverty to 24.3% in 2015.[8]

The COVID-19 pandemic and measures taken to contain it have resulted in a fall in remittances and tourism and the closure of many small and medium-sized enterprises (SMEs). Jobs and livelihoods have been put at severe risk, with unemployment rates reaching new highs in many countries. Rising food prices, reduced household incomes, and disrupted food supply chains exacerbate the risk of malnutrition among vulnerable and poor households. Progress toward gender equity goals is being further jeopardized as women have been called upon to provide even more unpaid care, their participation in the labor force has declined, and their risk of falling into poverty has heightened.[9] Children across the region have been out of school, and major disruptions to essential health services have meant that many children are missing out on crucial vaccinations among other impacts.[10]

---

[6]   ADB. 2020. The Impact of COVID-19 on Developing Asia: The Pandemic Extends into 2021.
[7]   ADB. 2020. Asian Development Outlook 2020 Update: Wellness in Worrying Times.
[8]   United Nations Development Programme. 2020. In Pakistan, Pandemic Could Push Millions more into Poverty.
[9]   United Nations. 2020. Policy Brief: The Impact of COVID-19 on Women.
[10]   United Nations Children's Fund (UNICEF). 2020. COVID-19: Children in Indonesia at Risk of Lifelong Consequences.

B. Institutionalizing the 2030 Agenda for Sustainable Development

ADB is increasingly embedding the SDGs across its planning and reporting mechanisms, including in the templates for reports and recommendations of the President for project approvals, country partnership strategies (CPSs), and regional partnership strategies. Figure 12 details the evolution of ADB's efforts to align its internal processes and policies with the SDGs. These iterative internal alignments aim to orient ADB operations to help countries make progress on the 2030 Agenda by delivering SDG-aligned results. Figure 3 presents the theory of change underlying ADB's approach to the SDGs, including its continuous efforts to strengthen the effectiveness and financial sustainability of ADB operations and build on long-standing support for its members' sustainable development needs.

Strategic alignment. Strategy 2030 and its associated corporate results framework (CRF), the operational plans for the seven Strategy 2030 operational priorities (Figure 4), the plans of ADB's sector and thematic groups, and the CPSs provide the fundamental underpinnings for aligning ADB's operations with the SDGs.

Alignment of operational priorities. The development of the Strategy 2030 operational plans and their ensuing implementation is enabled by interdepartmental sector and thematic working groups, each of which has an operational plan that relates to the SDGs.[11] Sector groups also develop work plans that relate to relevant SDGs. ADB's Operational Plan for Private Sector Operations, 2019–2024 identifies SDG-aligned priority areas, including a focus on sectors such as agribusiness, education, and health.[12] Features of these plans and associated policies that enable specific aspects of the SDGs are outlined in section II of this report.

ADB's aspirations for Asia and the Pacific are aligned with major global commitments that both DMCs and ADB have pledged to support—the SDGs and the related Financing for Development agenda, the Paris Agreement on Climate Change, and the Sendai Framework for Disaster Risk Reduction. ADB's future operations will be designed to help meet these goals and targets.

---

[11] ADB. 2018. Strategy 2030.
[12] ADB. 2019. Operational Plan for Private Sector Operations, 2019–2024.

ADB Internal SDG Alignment & Engagement

SDG alignment of key planning and reporting mechanisms	**Improved alignment of planning and reporting with SDGs:** PLANNING — S2030, CRF, 7 OPs/KMAP/etc., S/TG Frameworks, CPS, R/PS, COBP, RRPs REPORTING — SDG Corporate Report, DEfR, [7 OPs/ KMAP/etc.], [S/TG Reports], [CPS FRs], [Completion Reports]	RDs, PSOD, and SDCC plan and assist DMCs on SDG issues and implementation
PCS, DMF integrate SDGs	Enhanced systems and processes to track SDG alignment	Undertaking, commissioning, and partnering for SDG knowledge products
Convening periodic bank-wide coordination	Improved coordination and information sharing on SDGs across ADB	Convening key stakeholders on selected SDG topics
Delivery of training and capacity building on SDG topics	Increased understanding and focus on SDGs amon ADB staff	Increased ADB assistance (projects, programs, non-lending; SOV / NSO/ TA) principles of SDG
Undertaking SDG enabling research: acceleration, etc.	Accelerator criteria developed, refined, and applied	Coordinating MDBs, commissioning and undertaking research on SDGs and MDBs

Key ADB Topics:
- Regional SDG progress and prospects
- Social protection
- Natural capital and climate change
- Governance and localization
- Domestic resource mobilization
- Gender

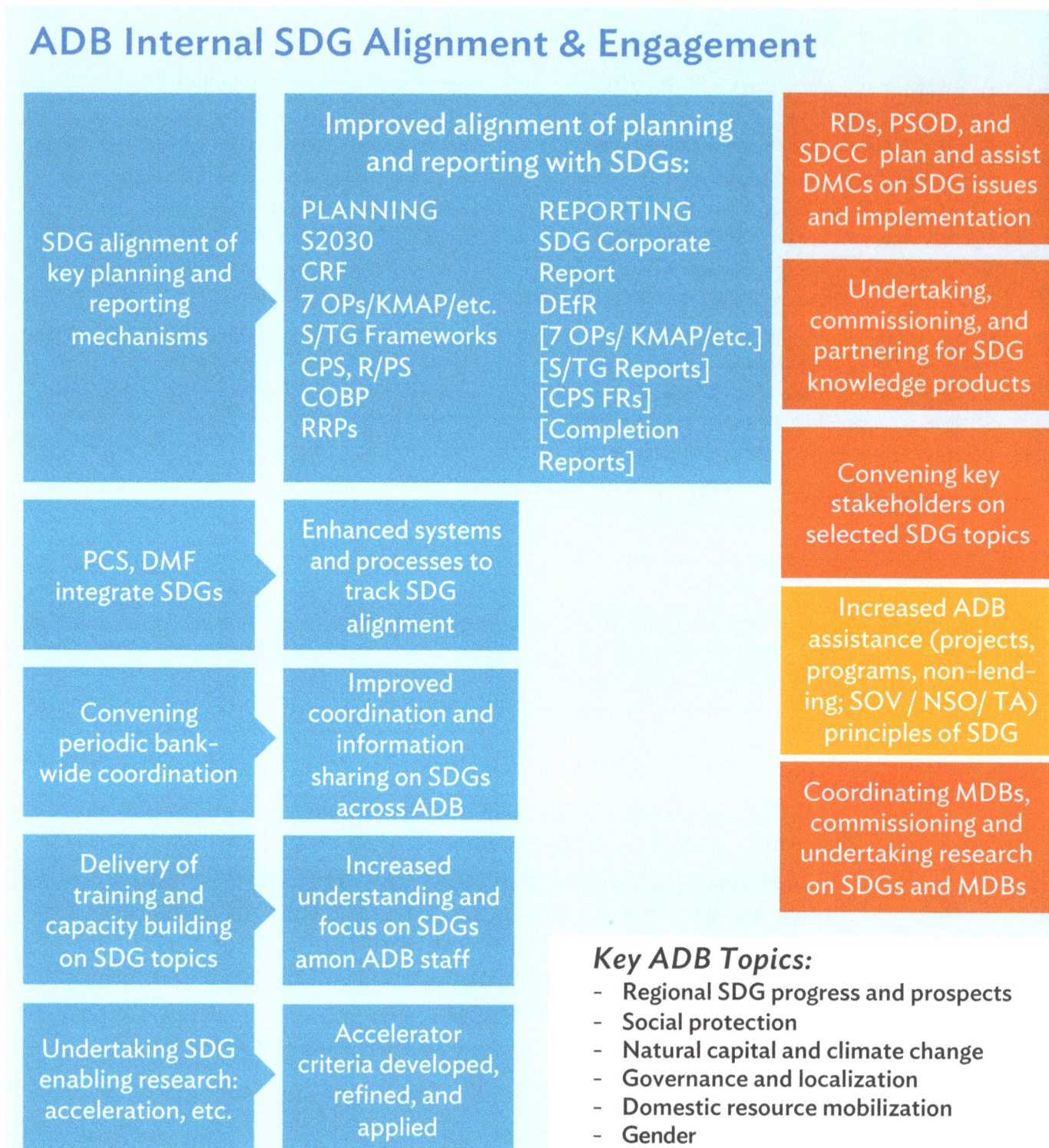

ADB = Asian Development Bank, COBP = country operations business plan, CPS = country partnership strategy, CRF = corporate results framework, DEfR = development effectiveness review, DMC = developing member country, DMF = design and monitoring framework, FR = framework review, KMAP = Knowledge Management Action Plan, MDB = multilateral development bank, NSO = nonsovereign operation, OP = operational priority, PCS = project classification system, PSOD = Private Sector Operations Department, RD = regional department, RPS = regional partnership strategy, RRP = report and recommendation of the President, S2030 = Strategy 2030, S/TG = sector and thematic groups, SDCC = Sustainable Development and Climate Change Department, SDG = Sustainable Development Goal, SOV = sovereign, TA = technical assistance, WG = working group.

DMC Achievement of SDGs

Supporting DMCs on SDG implementation

Improved knowledge and understanding of SDG issues in Asia and the Pacific among key audiences

(Leave no one behind, integrated solutions, innovation, mobilizing finance, partnerships)

Joint MDB approaches to SDG measurement and reporting

National and subnational SDG architecture strengthened	Improved integration of SDGs into national and subnational development plans
	Increased financing to support SDG attainment
	Improved data on SDG achievement

Increased achievement of SDG-aligned outcomes from ADB projects, including in context of COVID-19 recovery support

CONTRIBUTION TO SDG ATTAINMENT

ADB internal effort

ADB effort enabling country action

ADB operations

Country SDG progress

SDG aligned results

Source: Asian Development Bank.

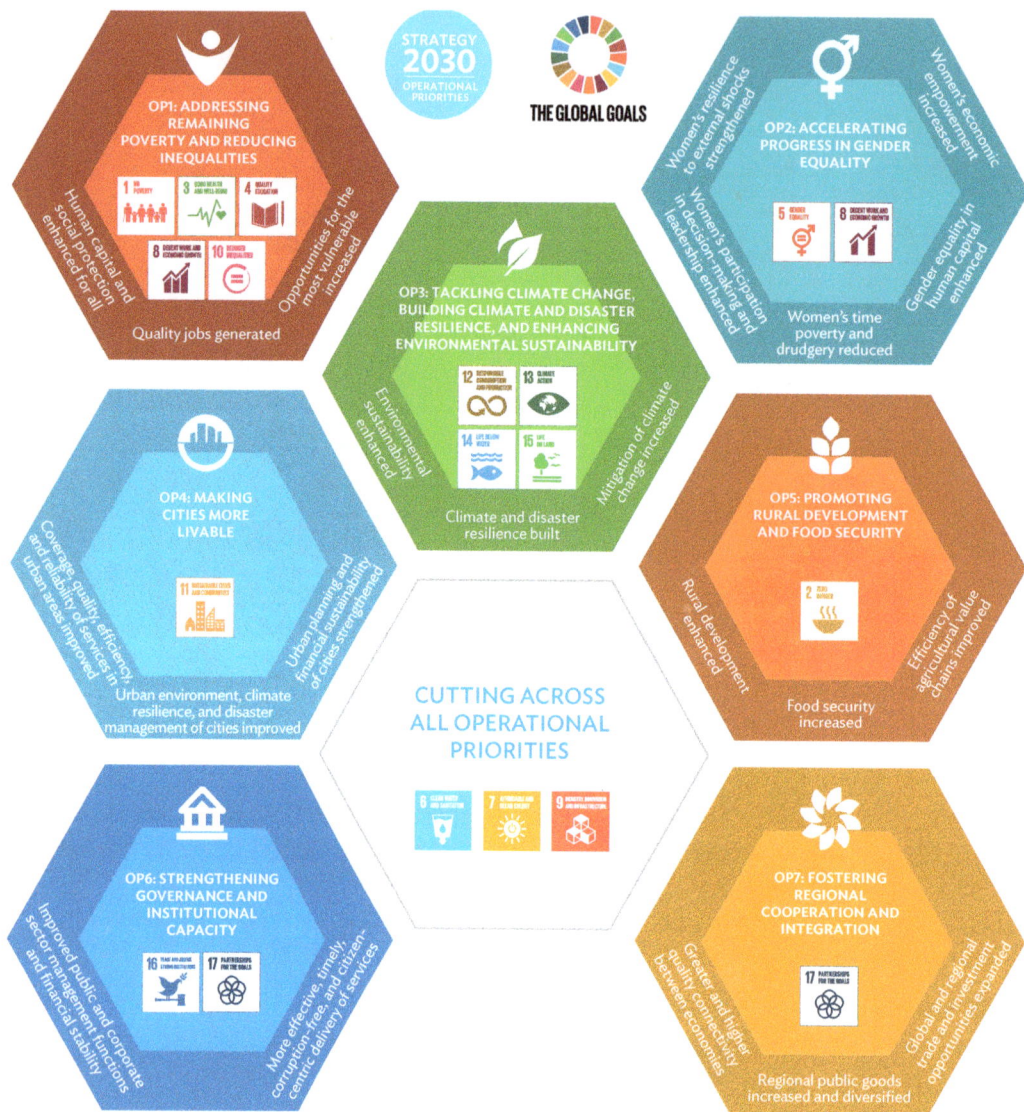

OP = operational priority.
Source: Asian Development Bank.

Corporate results framework alignment and typology. ADB uses its CRF 2019–2024 to assess the institution's operational and organizational performance with respect to the goals of Strategy 2030 (Figure 5).[13] Wherever possible and appropriate, ADB has related its CRF indicators to specific SDGs and associated targets. In so doing, it has developed a typology to characterize the relationship of its CRF indicators with the official SDG framework of targets and indicators (Box 1). The Organisation for Economic Co-operation and Development (OECD) has adapted this typology as a framework to help other development partners relate their results management framework indicators to the SDGs.[14] Selected results from completed ADB operations by SDG were presented in Appendix 2 of the *2019 Development Effectiveness Review* (footnote 3).

---

[13]   ADB. 2019. ADB Corporate Results Framework, 2019–2024.
[14]   OECD. 2020. Guiding Principles on Managing for Sustainable Development Results—Key Issues and Guidance to Support Implementation. Background paper: OECD Development Assistance Committee Results Community Workshop. 19 November.

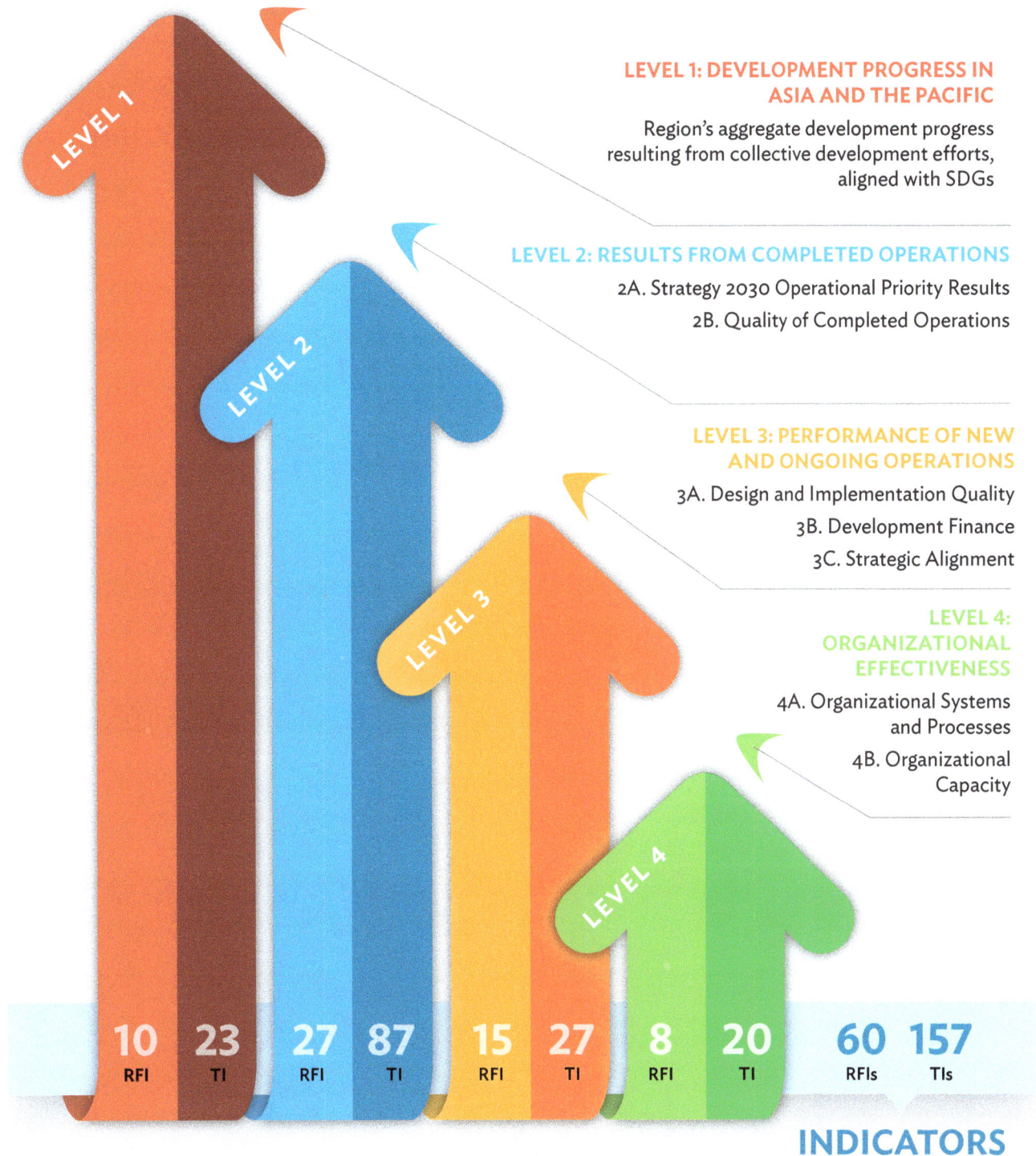

LEVEL 1: DEVELOPMENT PROGRESS IN ASIA AND THE PACIFIC

Region's aggregate development progress resulting from collective development efforts, aligned with SDGs

LEVEL 2: RESULTS FROM COMPLETED OPERATIONS

2A. Strategy 2030 Operational Priority Results

2B. Quality of Completed Operations

LEVEL 3: PERFORMANCE OF NEW AND ONGOING OPERATIONS

3A. Design and Implementation Quality

3B. Development Finance

3C. Strategic Alignment

LEVEL 4: ORGANIZATIONAL EFFECTIVENESS

4A. Organizational Systems and Processes

4B. Organizational Capacity

LEVEL 1		LEVEL 2		LEVEL 3		LEVEL 4			
10	23	27	87	15	27	8	20	60	157
RFI	TI	RFI	TI	RFI	TI	RFI	TI	RFIs	TIs

INDICATORS

RFI = results framework indicator, SDG = Sustainable Development Goal, TI = tracking indicator.

Country alignment. ADB has also begun to align its country engagement processes with the SDGs. For example, the Strategy 2030-aligned CPS template prompts attention to the progress against the SDGs and associated priorities. The CPS is ADB's primary platform for engaging with partner country government stakeholders around operational priorities to support planning and programming of country operations. Highlights of engagement on the SDGs in selected countries in the context of CPS development are featured in section II. To support CPS alignment with national SDG priorities, ADB has partnered with the United Nations Development Programme (UNDP) to develop a pilot set of SDG implementation snapshots in Armenia, Cambodia, Indonesia, Nepal, Pakistan, and Thailand, which synthesize the countries' efforts to act on the SDGs. Lessons from this pilot will be used to strengthen the approach.

Systems to track project links. ADB has integrated the SDGs into its project classification system and project design and monitoring frameworks to create systems that track projects' links to the SDGs. These links are noted in the project-at-a-glance summary included in reports and recommendations of the President for new ADB projects. While the electronic system supports tagging, project officers have substantial discretion to override default settings and relate projects to the SDGs and associated targets. The approach to linking projects to the SDGs is updated and refined periodically to reflect new institutional developments and learning from system rollout (Box 2).

Box 1: Relationship of ADB Corporate Results Framework Indicators to the Official Sustainable Development Goals Monitoring Framework

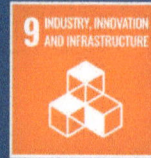

Direct use of Sustainable Development Goal (SDG) indicators in level 1 (Development Progress in Asia and the Pacific)

E.g., SDG indicator 9.4.1: carbon dioxide emissions per unit of gross domestic product

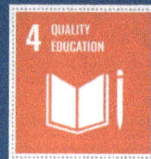

Derived Indicators in levels 2 and 3: Directly related to an official SDG indicator

E.g., people enrolled in improved education and/or training is derived from SDG indicator 4.3.1 with slight adaptation i.e., number of people vs. participation rate (%)

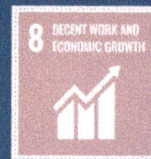

Aligned indicators in levels 1 to 3: Closely linked to SDG indicator or captures certain elements

E.g., Women opening new accounts aligns with SDG indicator 8.10.2: proportion of adults (15 years and older) with an account at a bank or other financial institution or with a mobile money service provider

Proxy indicators in levels 1 to 3: Relate to overall SDG objectives rather than to an official SDG indicator

E.g., People benefiting from improved services in urban areas (number)

Box 2: Linking Projects to the Sustainable Development Goals: ADB's Approach

The Sustainable Development Goals (SDGs) have been reflected in the project classification system of the Asian Development Bank (ADB) through e-Operations, an integrated information technology platform that manages all project-related information and documents, since 2016. The initial system was simply a list of all 17 SDGs that could be linked to as many or as few goals as project officers deemed relevant. This approach resulted in substantial variation in practice, both in terms of how many goals were selected, and on what basis.

ADB revised the project classification system in 2019 to make use of information already captured, such as subsector codes and strategic objective tags, to help shortlist SDG goals and targets that were most likely to be relevant to projects. It also adapted the system to try to capture the amount of financing that could be attributed to specific SDGs and targets. In the revised system, 100% of financing is split across relevant sector-driven goal targets. Up to 100% of financing can also be attributed to crosscutting SDG targets; i.e., SDG 1 (No Poverty—linked to poverty tagging), SDG 5 (Gender Equality—linked to gender mainstreaming), SDG 10 (Reduced Inequalities—linked to inclusive economic growth tagging to social protection systems), SDG 12 (Responsible Consumption and Production—prompted by tagging to environmentally sustainable growth). Climate finance is attributed to SDG 13 (Climate Action). Project officers can override the default finance distribution as needed. ADB is the first multilateral development bank (MDB) to have created such a system.

The system is revised and updated as needed to reflect strategic developments and user feedback. One important planned improvement is to triangulate SDG targets proposed by this input-driven tagging method with SDG targets related to indicators in project design and monitoring frameworks. ADB is also working closely with other MDBs through the MDB Working Group on Managing for Development Results to support common approaches to reporting on the SDGs. ADB will adapt and refine its approach to ensure consistency with evolving MDB practice and other development practice such as guidance from the Organisation for Economic Co-operation and Development on linking projects reported as Total Official Support for Sustainable Development.

Figure 6: 2019 ADB Projects Mapped to the Sustainable Development Goals

SECTOR-BASED GOALS

- 9 INDUSTRY, INNOVATION AND INFRASTRUCTURE — 29%
- 11 SUSTAINABLE CITIES AND COMMUNITIES — 18%
- 7 AFFORDABLE AND CLEAN ENERGY — 17%
- OTHER GOALS 2,4,14,15,16,17 — 27%
- 8 DECENT WORK AND ECONOMIC GROWTH — 16%
- 6 CLEAN WATER AND SANITATION — 15%
- 3 GOOD HEALTH AND WELL-BEING — 12%

CROSSCUTTING THEMATIC GOALS

- 13 CLIMATE ACTION — 62%
- 5 GENDER EQUALITY — 51%
- 10 REDUCED INEQUALITIES — 35%
- 1 NO POVERTY — 35%
- 12 RESPONSIBLE CONSUMPTION AND PRODUCTION — 15%

Source: Asian Development Bank. 2020. 2019 Development Effectiveness Review.

Internal coordination and exchange. ADB convenes periodic coordination discussions, as needed, to enable information sharing across the institution on efforts to support the agenda. The Results Management and Aid Effectiveness Division of the Strategy, Policy and Partnerships Department acts as ADB's focal point for the SDGs. ADB also supports training and capacity building workshops to increase internal awareness, understanding, and focus on the SDGs, with a view to strengthening the contributions of ADB projects to SDG attainment.

Operations and knowledge support. ADB's operations and knowledge departments assist DMCs on SDG implementation. Key dimensions of SDG implementation include establishing an effective architecture to support delivery of the SDGs within countries, integrating the SDGs into national plans and setting priorities to this end, delivering finance for projects and programs that will support progress on the SDGs alongside wider reforms and innovations to mobilize the finance necessary to achieve them, and developing the data and monitoring systems necessary to track and assess progress toward the SDGs.

ADB commissions, undertakes, and partners with other organizations to create knowledge on a diverse range of themes and issues that support progress toward the SDGs. It also convenes stakeholders on SDG-related issues. For example, ADB supports regional policy dialogue on SDG progress in collaboration with the United Nations (UN) and other partners. ADB's sector and thematic groups lead diverse knowledge and convening efforts that also support exchange and learning that is directly linked to progress on the SDGs, such as the Asia Clean Energy Forum, the Asia Finance Forum, and the Asia and the Pacific Transport Forum. Section II reviews SDG-focused knowledge and capacity building programs, including key knowledge partnerships.

Coordination with partners. In addition, ADB works with other MDBs through the MDB Working Group on Managing for Development Results to advance collective engagement on the SDGs, ensure alignment, and advance common approaches to measuring and reporting on the SDGs. It also engages with other development partners on SDG alignment at global and regional forums. ADB's resident missions promote effective development cooperation at the country level to achieve the SDGs. Examples include coordinating multi-donor trust funds, such as the Afghanistan Infrastructure Trust Fund, and cochairing development cooperation mechanisms such as the Development Partner Facility in Cambodia and the Cooperation Partners Group in Myanmar. ADB also works closely with partners in the UN system, particularly through a partnership between ESCAP, ADB, and UNDP to support regional progress on the SDGs, and partnerships with UNDP to leverage knowledge in the UN system to support SDG implementation and financing at the country level. These collaborations are detailed in section II.

The combined efforts described in the preceding paragraphs help deepen ADB's support for country implementation of the SDGs and scale up ADB operations that advance the 2030 Agenda for Sustainable Development.

II. Highlights of ADB's Support for the 2030 Agenda

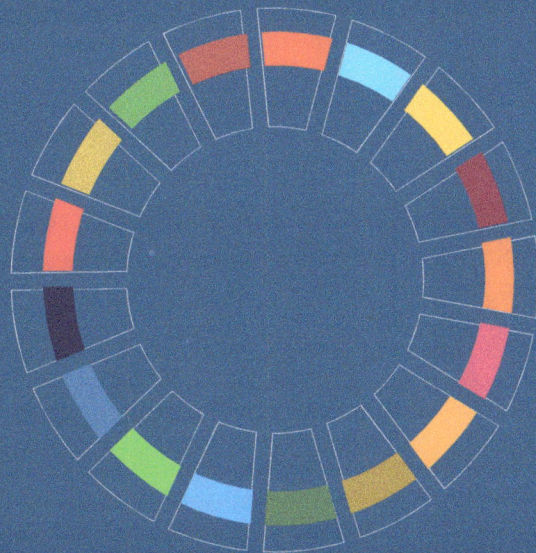

Figure 7: How does ADB support the SDGs in Asia and the Pacific?

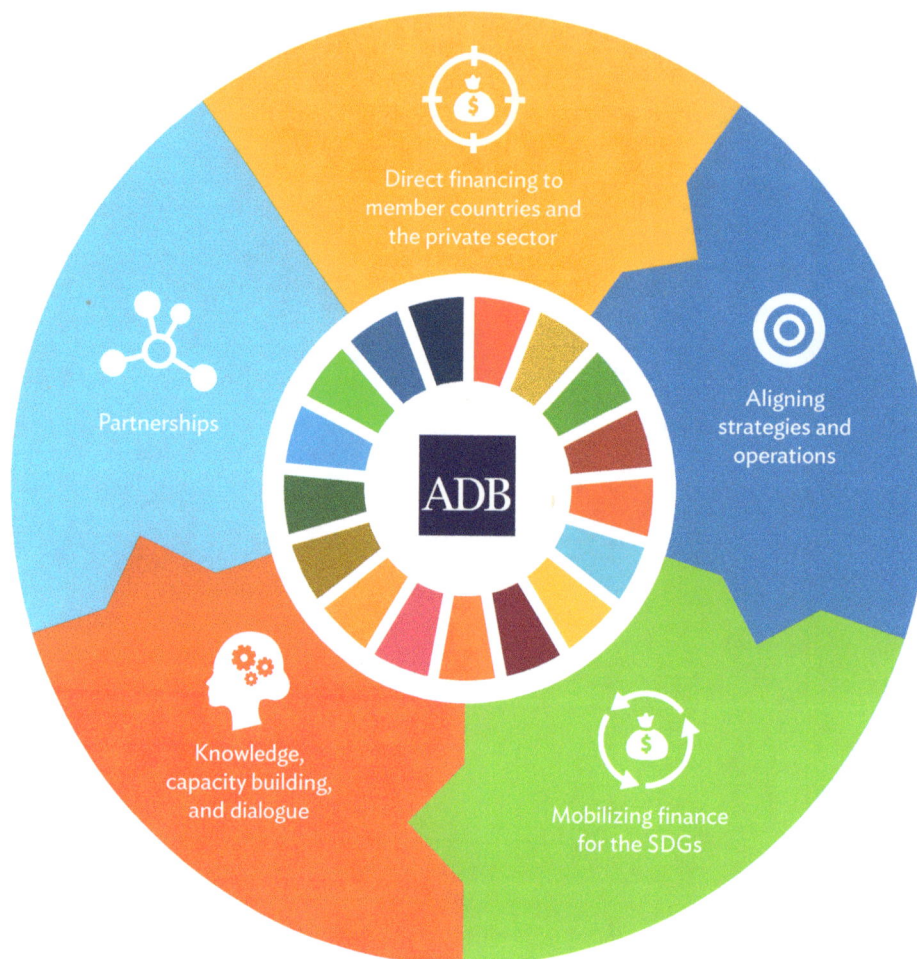

Most ADB projects have direct links to multiple SDGs and associated targets (Figure 6), and there are many more indirect links between ADB projects and the SDGs. This section draws out key features of ADB's support for SDG implementation in the DMCs and in the overall region in the context of Strategy 2030 priorities. It is organized around the four interlinked themes anchored in the 2030 Agenda for Sustainable Development and the Addis Ababa Action Agenda on financing for development: people, planet, prosperity, and sustainable infrastructure. These clusters, like the SDGs themselves, relate to each other in many ways. The fifth theme of this section highlights ADB's support for partnerships for finance and knowledge, which contribute to SDG 17: Partnerships for the Goals.

The projects featured in this section were approved after the SDGs came into force on 1 January 2016. They are firmly anchored in the official SDG framework of goals, targets, and indicators, and have been identified by ADB's sector and thematic groups and operations departments as having a strong rooting in the agenda. The projects take a holistic approach to sustainable development by addressing multiple SDGs and at least two of the three social, economic, and environmental dimensions of sustainable development. They also include features that reflect the ambitions of the 2030 Agenda, such as a focus on the needs of the most vulnerable to leave no one behind; partnerships that attract, mobilize, or catalyze additional financing for the SDGs; and/or other factors that will enable the project or program to be scaled up or replicated.

A. People

New life. A mother looks over her newborn in a hospital in the Kyrgyz Republic (photo by Rasanakunov Kanat Djaparovich).

Figure 8: ADB Support for People-Related Sustainable Development Goals in 2019

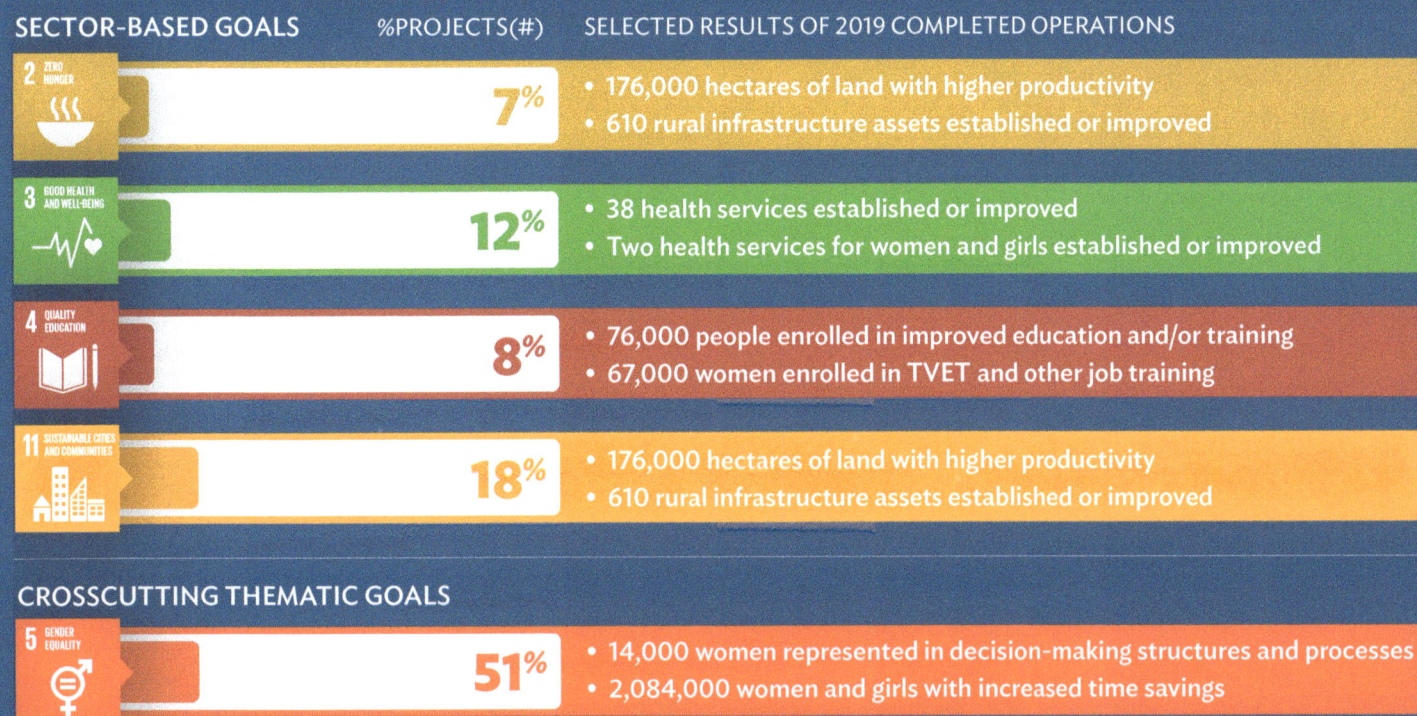

SECTOR-BASED GOALS

	%PROJECTS(#)	SELECTED RESULTS OF 2019 COMPLETED OPERATIONS
2 ZERO HUNGER	**7%**	• 176,000 hectares of land with higher productivity • 610 rural infrastructure assets established or improved
3 GOOD HEALTH AND WELL-BEING	**12%**	• 38 health services established or improved • Two health services for women and girls established or improved
4 QUALITY EDUCATION	**8%**	• 76,000 people enrolled in improved education and/or training • 67,000 women enrolled in TVET and other job training
11 SUSTAINABLE CITIES AND COMMUNITIES	**18%**	• 176,000 hectares of land with higher productivity • 610 rural infrastructure assets established or improved

CROSSCUTTING THEMATIC GOALS

	%PROJECTS(#)	
5 GENDER EQUALITY	**51%**	• 14,000 women represented in decision-making structures and processes • 2,084,000 women and girls with increased time savings

TVET = technical and vocational education and training.

Source: Asian Development Bank. 2020. 2019 Development Effectiveness Review: Scorecard and Related Information.

19

1. Context

Regional progress. Investing in human capital and ensuring access to services that allow people to realize their full potential is imperative. These efforts are closely related to the SDGs focused on promoting prosperity and eradicating poverty in all its forms, discussed further in section II C. Asia and Pacific DMCs have been working to expand access to health care. The quality of universal health coverage service coverage has improved, although coverage remains incomplete and uneven (footnote 3). Realizing the economic potential of women can drive prosperity, yet only 50% of women participate in the formal labor force and gender pay gaps persist. Women have had to take on even more unpaid care and have been affected in many other ways by the COVID-19 pandemic. Educational enrollment rates in the region made significant progress although lower secondary graduation rates stagnated, and there is a recognized need to focus on the quality of educational attainment and equipping people with the skills needed to thrive in fast-changing economies. Despite improvements, food security remains a major challenge, highlighted by disruptions caused by the COVID-19 pandemic. In 2016, about 489 million people remained undernourished and about 20% of children under the age of 5 were stunted.[15] Rural–urban transitions across the region complicate efforts to ensure social inclusion and realize human potential. COVID-19 has posed major challenges in all these areas, highlighting glaring gaps in social protection systems and food insecurity.

Key features of ADB's approach. The SDGs commit to end poverty and hunger and to ensure that all human beings can fulfill their potential in dignity, equality, and in a healthy environment. Strategy 2030, in turn, envisions an inclusive Asia and the Pacific where extreme poverty is eradicated. ADB's first operational priority of Strategy 2030 aims to address remaining poverty and reduce inequalities by increasing the emphasis on human development and social inclusion, facilitating quality job creation, improving education, achieving better health for all, and strengthening social protection systems and service delivery for those in need.

ADB helps its DMCs reduce hunger; enhance the efficiency, productivity, and sustainability of their agriculture; and ensure food safety for their citizens through programming related to operational priority 5—promoting rural development and food security. Operational priority 2 promotes gender equality, both by encouraging gender mainstreaming throughout ADB's operations—setting an ambitious target that at least 75% of ADB's committed sovereign and nonsovereign operations will support gender equality by 2030—and through a strong focus on women's empowerment, as envisioned in SDG 5. ADB's fourth operational priority promotes livable cities in a rapidly urbanizing region, emphasizing the need for integrated solutions to realize green, competitive, resilient, and inclusive cities that address the social dimensions of urbanization, such as human centered design, and the particular needs of women, aging populations, people with disabilities, and migrants.

Investing in human capital is inextricable from efforts to eradicate poverty.

---

[15]   ESCAP, ADB, and UNDP. 2019. Fast-tracking the SDGs: Driving Asia-Pacific Transformations.

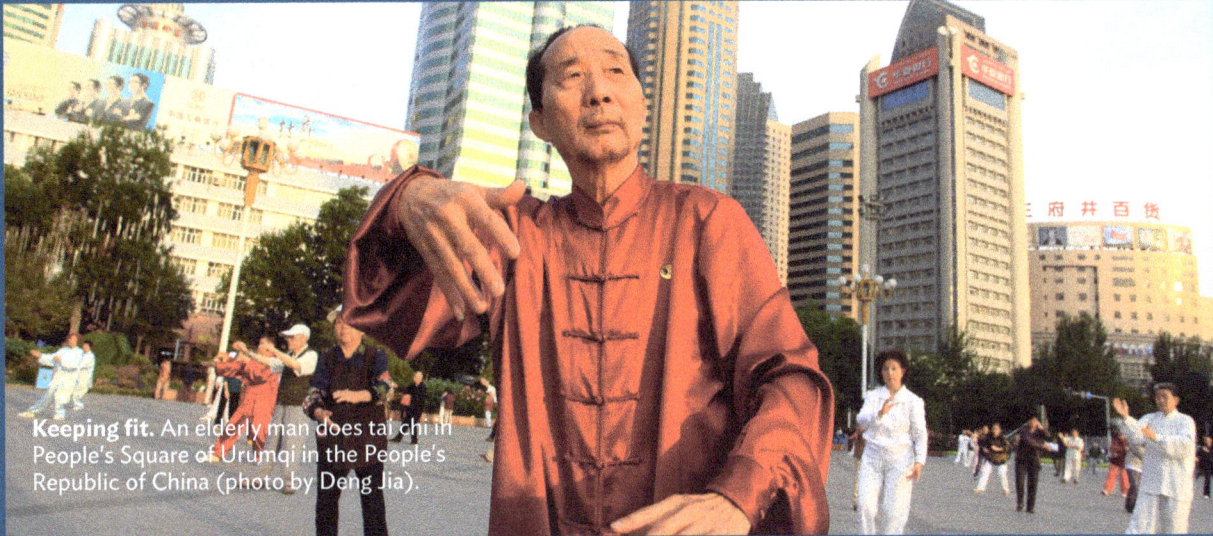

Keeping fit. An elderly man does tai chi in People's Square of Urumqi in the People's Republic of China (photo by Deng Jia).

Box 3: Leaving No One Behind: Supporting Older People

The People's Republic of China (PRC) is facing a major transition in its demographic structure. In 2017, 158 million people—11% of the population—were aged 65 years and above, and the elderly share of the population is projected to reach 14% in 2025 and 21% in 2035. At the same time, rapid urbanization, increased migration, and expanded female labor market participation have eroded traditional family support systems for the elderly.

Through the Hubei Yichang Comprehensive Elderly Care Demonstration Project, the Asian Development Bank (ADB) is working with the Yichang Municipal Government to establish a comprehensive, three-tiered elderly care service. The project will improve home- and community-based care services and facilities, including for elderly people suffering dementia; build a geriatric hospital and nursing home; and help develop a management scheme to ensure proper services and monitoring.

ADB is also supporting the Demonstration of Guangxi Elderly Care and Health Care Integration and Public–Private Partnership Project to establish an elderly care facility in Hezhou Municipality and improve coordinated care services and facilities in the municipalities of Hezhou and Nanning. The project will build four elderly care facilities and a medical institution with age-friendly designs and will showcase how coordinated care can be developed to provide better long-term services for the elderly. This is the first initiative in Guangxi Zhuang Autonomous Region to use public–private partnership principles and standards for elderly care.

Source: Asian Development Bank.

2. Investing in Human Capital: Health and Education

Support for education (SDG 4) and health (SDG 3) throughout people's lives as their needs change is fundamental to human capital development. Box 3 highlights how ADB is supporting the elderly, a vulnerable group targeted under operational priority 1. ADB has also created systems to track its efforts to target other vulnerable groups, such as people with disabilities. It supports diverse knowledge work aimed at helping countries identify opportunities to understand and manage changing demographics.[16]

---

[16]   See, for example, ADB. 2019. Asian Economic Integration Report 2019/2020: Demographic Change, Productivity, and the Role of Technology.

In Bhutan, ADB is helping to improve health services, especially in underserved areas. Aligned with Bhutan's efforts to progress toward universal health coverage based on the principles of primary health care, the Health Sector Development Program aims to establish five satellite clinics on the outskirts of urban areas, upgrade primary health care facilities, provide medical equipment, improve quality assurance, and promote healthy behavior changes. The program includes policy measures to enhance disease surveillance, develop a national e-health strategy, and achieve equitable health financing and a sustainable Bhutan Health Trust Fund with a core mandate to finance vaccines and essential medicines.

The adoption of digital health information systems also strengthens health care systems. In Tonga, the Introducing eGovernment through Digital Health Project aims to improve health services delivery by helping the government develop a gender-sensitive digital health strategy and improve legislation, policies, and regulations related to the health sector and the use of digital solutions. Such solutions can help better manage patient care, collect data for strategic decision-making, and track progress toward universal health coverage.

The COVID-19 pandemic has prompted ADB to substantially scale up its health sector engagement and mitigate the impact of the pandemic on SDG 3, as described in Box 4.

Box 4: ADB's Health Sector Response to Coronavirus Disease

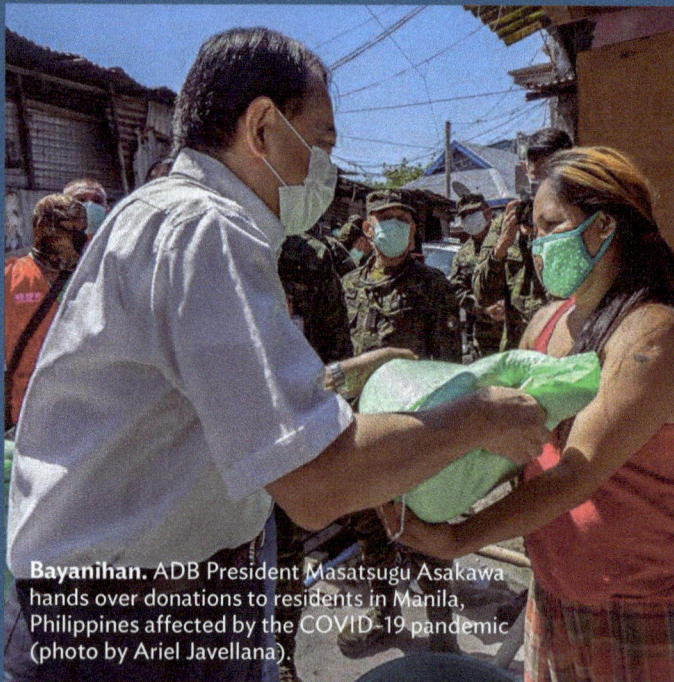

Bayanihan. ADB President Masatsugu Asakawa hands over donations to residents in Manila, Philippines affected by the COVID-19 pandemic (photo by Ariel Javellana).

As the development of coronavirus disease (COVID-19) vaccines progressed, the Asian Development Bank (ADB) has allocated $20.3 million in technical assistance to help its developing member countries (DMCs) access the vaccines and establish systems to enable equitable and efficient vaccine distribution. In collaboration with the COVID-19 Vaccines Global Access Facility (COVAX), Gavi, the United Nations Children's Fund (UNICEF), the World Bank, the World Health Organization, and other partners, ADB is helping its DMCs conduct vaccine-related health system assessments and develop country readiness plans to strengthen their capacity to access, introduce, and safely deploy and deliver vaccines, and to monitor their rollout effectively.

In late 2020, ADB also launched the Asia Pacific Vaccine Access Facility, a $9 billion initiative to help the DMCs procure vaccines. The program includes a rapid response component that provides timely support for critical vaccine diagnostics, procurement, and transport from the place of purchase to the DMCs; and a project investment component to support investments in systems for delivery and administration of vaccines along with associated investments in capacity building, community outreach, and surveillance. The program may also help develop or expand vaccine manufacturing capacity in the DMCs.

Source: Asian Development Bank.

Education is also a key element of ADB's support for human capital development. Quality education is an important enabler of progress across the SDGs, helping to foster entrepreneurship, industrial transformation, investment policy, and more sustainable urban development. Several recent ADB projects have focused on the intersection of innovation, technology, and skills development in sectors such as agriculture and health. Education is also a catalyst for the digital transformation that many countries are pursuing. ADB makes extensive investments in technical and vocational education and training in the context of its efforts to support decent jobs, which are discussed further in relation to ADB's contributions to SDGs linked to prosperity.

In Armenia, ADB is assisting the government's efforts to reform education and health services with a focus on helping women and girls. The Human Development Enhancement Program is helping the government lay the foundations to improve access to education and health services, remove structural impediments affecting the quality of services, improve financing and sector management, and promote healthy practices among children. Policy actions under this program will help expand preschool education coverage by adopting alternative preschool models, including community-based services. To improve the quality of education, new standards are being set for teachers, including teacher performance monitoring and evaluation mechanisms.

The Sindh Secondary Education Improvement Project will construct secondary school blocks, in the most deprived districts in southern Sindh Province, Pakistan. These will feature solar power and gender-segregated sanitation facilities and prayer rooms. A notable part of this project is the education management organizations (EMO) program, under which the government contracts private partners to operate public schools. Although the EMO-operated schools are privately managed, students do not pay fees. The government's payments to the EMOs are contingent on their performance against key indicators such as school management, teacher attendance, student enrollments, curriculum delivery, and staff professional development. The EMO program's performance-based approach facilitates effective learning outcomes while maintaining free provision of education services to secondary students in deprived areas.

3. Striving for Zero Hunger

Access to safe, nutritious, and affordable food is essential for people's well-being. A key element of ADB's support in this area is improving market connectivity and agricultural value chain links through the adoption of technology solutions. For example, in the People's Republic of China (PRC), ADB is leveraging information technology for food traceability and a two-way automated information exchange system between farmers and consumers. The Gansu Internet-Plus Agriculture Development Project is integrating an application of network-connected technology along the entire value chain from production to marketing. This will allow consumers to obtain product information and farmers to access market information and production support services to help them tap into high-value e-commerce markets.

ADB's investments also help boost farmer incomes and improve rural livelihoods. In Indonesia, Papua New Guinea, Timor-Leste, and Viet Nam, ADB's nonsovereign loan for the Agricultural Value Chain Development Project is supporting Olam International Limited and its subsidiaries, Café Outspan Vietnam Limited and PT Dharmapala Usaha Sukses, to improve agricultural value chains and bring significant positive impacts to farmers and the agribusiness industry. ADB's assistance enables Olam to increase its sourcing volumes from smallholder farmers. The project also leverages Olam's sustainability programs to provide agricultural extension services, training, and livelihood support to smallholder farmers.

Future scientist. A student conducting an experiment in the genetic engineering laboratory of the National University of Mongolia (photo by Eric Sales).

4. Promoting Gender Equality

Gender equality is central to ADB's work to reduce poverty in Asia and the Pacific. ADB has been working with its DMCs to eliminate barriers that make it difficult for women to thrive. To support this effort, ADB adopted gender mainstreaming categories for its projects in 2012 (Box 5). Concessional resources from the Asian Development Fund's 13th replenishment are also available for investments that promote progress on SDG 5 and support a transformative agenda for women. Regional technical assistance for Promoting Transformative Gender Equality Agenda in Asia and the Pacific helps governments and financial institutions introduce gender-responsive policy measures, train women entrepreneurs, and collect and disseminate data on women-owned small and medium-sized enterprises (SMEs). The program is cofinanced by the Women Entrepreneurs Finance Initiative and JP Morgan Chase & Co. and supports the Small and Medium-Sized Enterprises Line of Credit Project, which facilitates access to finance for women-led SMEs in Sri Lanka. ADB has provided long-term financing through 10 local participating banks to targeted SMEs in the country, using incentives and penalties to promote financial inclusion and set requirements for onlending to women-led SMEs. The Japan Fund for Poverty Reduction financed a complementary technical assistance grant that supports business development and financial literacy training for women entrepreneurs in promising export-generating sectors and awareness raising on entrepreneurship in information and communication technology. The Women Entrepreneurs Finance Initiative provided additional financing to expand the gender dimensions of the project, addressing a range of issues including limited access to finance and weaknesses in the market, policy, and regulatory environment.

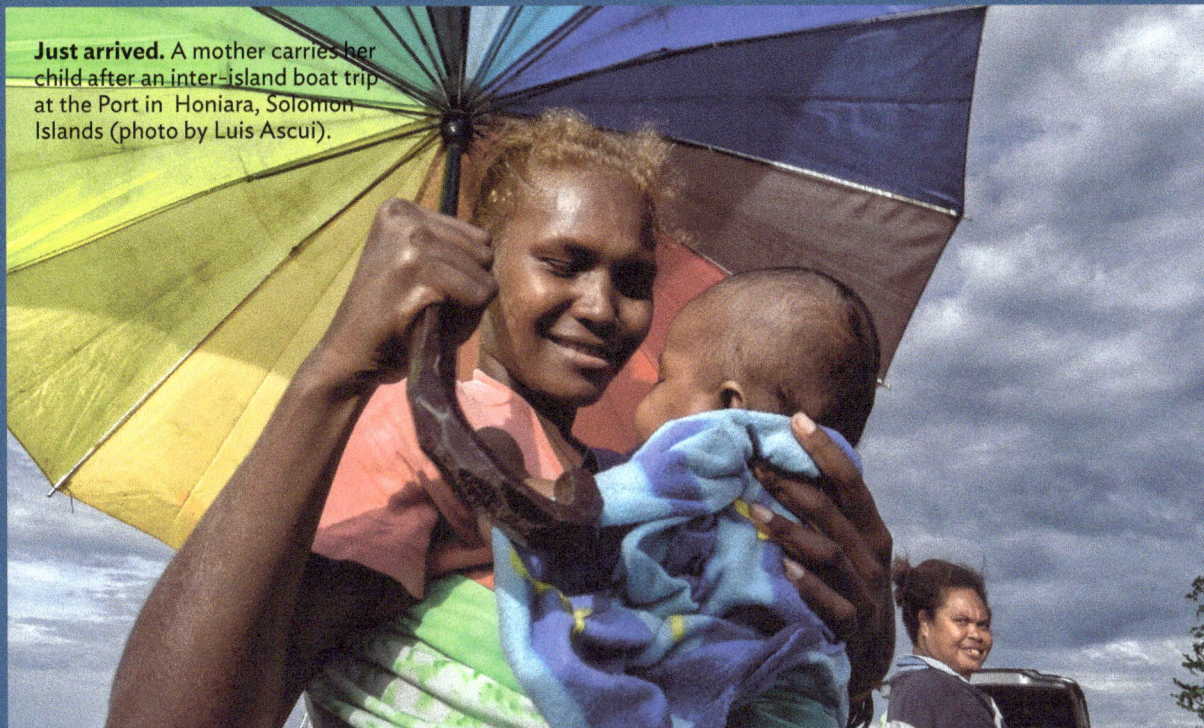

Just arrived. A mother carries her child after an inter-island boat trip at the Port in Honiara, Solomon Islands (photo by Luis Ascui).

Box 5: ADB's Approach to Gender Mainstreaming

The Asian Development Bank (ADB) adopted gender mainstreaming categories in 2012 as a key measure to promote gender equality and women's empowerment in all ADB operations, and to define, clarify, and make more tangible the concept of gender mainstreaming to ensure ADB-wide consistency in its application. All projects need to be assigned one of the following categories:

- *Gender equity theme.* The project outcome directly addresses gender equality and/or women's empowerment by narrowing gender disparities.

- *Effective gender mainstreaming.* The project outcomes are designed to deliver tangible benefits to women by directly improving their access to resources, services, opportunities, infrastructure, or by enhancing their voices and rights.

- *Some gender elements*. The project is likely to improve women's access to services, opportunities, and improved voice, or significant efforts were made to include some gender features to enhance benefits for women.

- *No gender elements*. The project outcome is not expected to provide direct or tangible benefits to women and girls during the project period. However, indirect benefits could be derived in the longer term.

ADB projects categorized *gender mainstreaming* (gender equity theme or effective gender mainstreaming) require a gender action plan and gender targets and indicators in the project design and monitoring framework to ensure women's participation and benefits. Key aspects of the gender action plan are incorporated into project assurances. Tool kits support design of the gender action plan and gender indicators and targets relevant to the specific subsector context.

Source: ADB. 2012. Guidelines for Gender Mainstreaming Categories of ADB Projects.

Given the size of its infrastructure portfolio, ADB has played an instrumental role in helping DMCs make infrastructure development more gender-inclusive. In Bangladesh, the Third Urban Governance and Infrastructure Improvement (Sector) Project seeks to strengthen urban governance and improve urban infrastructure and service delivery in 36 *pourashavas* (municipalities). The project supports the improvement of a wide range of infrastructure subprojects that are designed with gender- and climate-responsive features. This is coupled with building the capacity of *pourashavas* in urban service delivery, planning, and financial management, and inclusion of the poor and women in local governance. The adoption of targets for women's representation in committees for town and ward coordination, women's and children's affairs, and poverty reduction and slum improvement enables women to be part of municipal governance-related processes and structures. Gender equity and social inclusion is one of the pillars of the Urban Governance Improvement Action Program that all participating *pourashavas* need to fulfill.

ADB also integrates gender considerations in its policy-based lending to DMCs. For example, the Sustained Private Sector-Led Growth Reform Program is helping Fiji create greater private investment opportunities and improve the business and investment climate. The program also aims to improve public financial management and strengthen the performance of state-owned enterprises. The loan includes policy actions that will promote gender equality, women's economic empowerment, and women's access to resources and services such as support for SMEs owned or led by women and direct cash transfers to informal workers, including for women-owned microenterprises.

The program also supported an assessment of the gender impacts of COVID-19 in Fiji and drafting of a guidance note, which was presented to the cabinet, and the establishment of a COVID-19 gender working group to implement the recommendations of the guidance note. Reforms under this program will expand gender-responsive budgeting in government programs and ensure that future COVID-19 programs include targeted measures for women's economic empowerment.

Recognizing that women and girls in poor and low-income households are among those most severely affected by the pandemic, all ADB programs under the COVID-19 Pandemic Response Option incorporate strong gender dimensions. Supported programs covered social assistance, economic stimulus measures, and health sector support in which women were specifically targeted. As the lockdowns imposed in response to COVID-19 have also increased the vulnerability of women and girls to domestic violence, ADB has worked with its DMCs to provide resources for programs to combat gender-based violence.

ADB also invests in knowledge to support progress on gender equality across the SDGs. For example, ADB partnered with UN Women's regional office for Asia and the Pacific to develop comprehensive baselines for SDG targets related to gender equality across the SDGs, and opportunities to promote women's empowerment in the region.

Empowering women and girls is central to achieving the SDGs and a focus of Strategy 2030.

5. Livable Cities and Sustainable Urban Communities

Asia's rapid pace of urbanization is creating an imperative for deeper engagement to foster more inclusive and sustainable cities.[17] Through strategic operational priority 4, ADB supports crosscutting projects in cities that promote health, mobility, gender equality, climate resilience, and environmental sustainability, with a focus on water, sanitation, waste disposal services, sustainable public transport, and connectivity. Policy and institutional support is a critical element of these efforts.

Investments in two cities in Pakistan illustrate this approach. Through the Punjab Intermediate Cities Improvement Investment Project, ADB's assistance will enhance public spaces by rehabilitating parks and improving city public transport routes and footpaths with traffic signals at road crossings, adaptive traffic control, and bus terminals in the cities of Sahiwal and Sialkot. In addition, the project will improve water supply and sanitation, targeting special distribution network zones where vulnerable groups live and increasing the volume of treated wastewater. This will promote better living standards for residents and improve public health while also strengthening business processes and economic activities.

The Phuentsholing Township Development Project in Bhutan is another example of ADB's holistic approach to urban development and resilience. ADB helped the government incorporate social, economic, environmental, and physical aspects in the township master plan during project preparation to support inclusive and integrated urban planning. The project community was engaged to develop management plans to protect residents against climate risks such as floods and riverbank erosion.

In Myanmar, the Third Greater Mekong Subregion Corridor Towns Development Project aims to help upgrade the water distribution network and solid waste management infrastructure in the towns of Mawlamyine in Mon State, and Hpa-An and Myawaddy in Kayin State. It also involves the conservation of heritage sites and development of a joint spatial development plan for two towns at the Myanmar–Thailand border. The improved basic social infrastructure and urban services are expected to yield health and economic gains that will benefit the residents.

ADB manages several donor trust funds to provide the concessional finance some DMCs need to help remove the integrated impediments to making cities more livable. For example, the ASEAN Australia Smart Cities Trust Fund,[18] established in April 2019 under the Urban Financing Partnership Facility, supports activities that will help participating cities adapt and adopt digital solutions and governance systems. ADB also participates in knowledge sharing and networking initiatives such as the Global Platform for Sustainable Cities. Coordinated by the World Bank, the platform works with a core group of 23 cities to provide access to cutting-edge urban planning and management tools and promotes integrated approaches to planning and financing.

---

[17] ADB. 2019. Asian Development Outlook Update: Fostering Growth and Inclusion in Asia's Cities.
[18] The fund focuses on building livable cities that are green, competitive, inclusive, and resilient, reflecting the ASEAN (Association of Southeast Asian Nations) Sustainable Urbanization Strategy, which aims to promote a high quality of life, competitive economies, and sustainable environments.

Spotlight: Mongolia

Mongolia was one of the first countries to reflect the Sustainable Development Goals (SDGs) in its national agenda through the Mongolia Sustainable Development Vision 2030.

In 2018, the Asian Development Bank (ADB) partnered with the United Nations Development Programme to support Mongolia in the development of an SDGs mainstreaming, acceleration, and policy support assessment to identify priorities for SDG implementation in the country, the findings of which were presented to government counterparts. The National Statistics Office has carried out data readiness assessments on SDG monitoring and has created the SDG Dashboard with international partners. Mongolia is identifying national indicators and targets through sub-working groups for SDG indicators established in 2019, which will be integrated with the SDG Dashboard.

ADB's country partnership strategy for Mongolia, 2017–2020 addresses key sustainable development challenges by supporting investments, policy reforms, capacity building, and knowledge sharing to sustain inclusive growth in a period of economic difficulty. It focuses on infrastructure gaps, renewable energy, regional economic integration, access to urban services, and agribusiness.

ADB's support to Mongolia exemplifies the crosscutting nature of the 2030 Agenda, and the importance of supporting countries across sectors. The Improving Access to Health Services for Disadvantaged Groups Investment Program, ADB's first multitranche financing facility in Mongolia, aims to provide high-quality health care services in selected disadvantaged *ger* (traditional tent) areas of Ulaanbaatar, the provinces, and subdistricts as part of the national commitment to universal health coverage.

The Ulaanbaatar Green Affordable Housing and Resilient Urban Renewal Sector Project aims to deliver 10,000 affordable green housing units. ADB is collaborating with the International Finance Corporation and the local government to support the implementation of the Excellence for Design and Greater Efficiencies green building standards and certification system for the program.

The Sustainable Tourism Development Project supports ecotourism and national park sustainability for two globally important protected areas in Khuvsgul and Khentii aimags (provinces), and protection of the country's most important freshwater resource, Khuvsgul Lake. The project will upgrade tourism infrastructure and improve park management to safeguard wilderness areas.

The Upscaling Renewable Energy Sector Project is developing a 41-megawatt distributed renewable energy system to supply power and heating in the country's remote and less developed western regions. The project will also prepare a long-term renewable energy investment plan for Mongolia, including an energy policy and regulatory framework amendments to support private-sector-led development.

In 2019, ADB approved a $7.5 million private sector loan to expand the dairy production of Mongolia's leading food and beverage company. Smallholder farmers and herders, who are the company's main suppliers, will be the beneficiaries of the Gender Inclusive Dairy Value Chain Project.

ADB has also developed its first dedicated project to address domestic violence in Mongolia. The Combating Domestic Violence Against Women and Children Project will establish shelters, develop institutional capacity, improve prevention and reporting, and empower women survivors by supporting livelihoods and income generation.

ADB is supporting Mongolia to address the SDGs through investments, policy reforms, capacity building, and knowledge sharing to sustain inclusive growth.

Progress on Selected Indicators

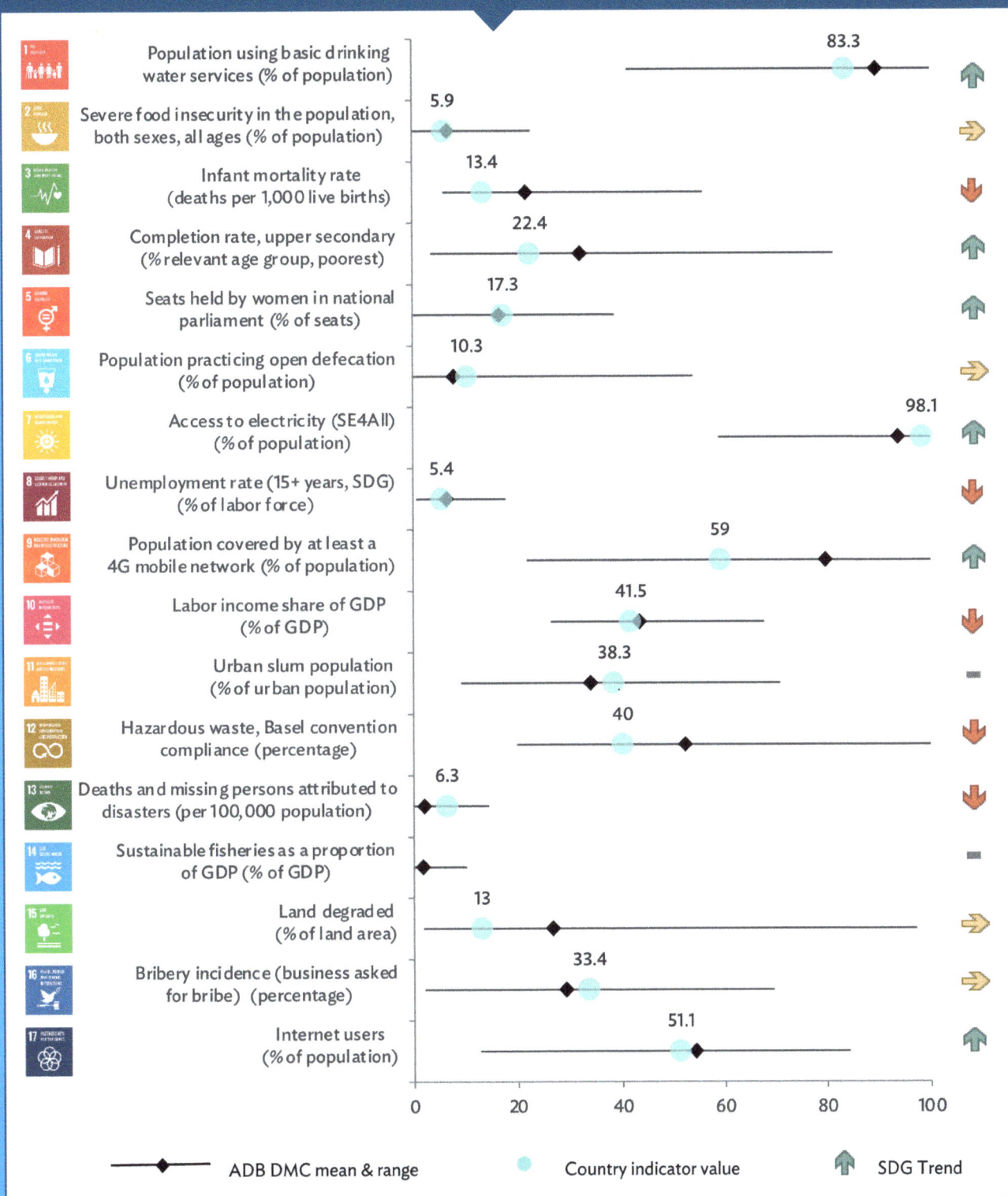

SDG	Indicator	Value	Trend
1	Population using basic drinking water services (% of population)	83.3	⬆
2	Severe food insecurity in the population, both sexes, all ages (% of population)	5.9	➡
3	Infant mortality rate (deaths per 1,000 live births)	13.4	⬇
4	Completion rate, upper secondary (% relevant age group, poorest)	22.4	⬆
5	Seats held by women in national parliament (% of seats)	17.3	⬆
6	Population practicing open defecation (% of population)	10.3	➡
7	Access to electricity (SE4All) (% of population)	98.1	⬆
8	Unemployment rate (15+ years, SDG) (% of labor force)	5.4	⬇
9	Population covered by at least a 4G mobile network (% of population)	59	⬆
10	Labor income share of GDP (% of GDP)	41.5	⬇
11	Urban slum population (% of urban population)	38.3	—
12	Hazardous waste, Basel convention compliance (percentage)	40	⬇
13	Deaths and missing persons attributed to disasters (per 100,000 population)	6.3	⬇
14	Sustainable fisheries as a proportion of GDP (% of GDP)		—
15	Land degraded (% of land area)	13	➡
16	Bribery incidence (business asked for bribe) (percentage)	33.4	➡
17	Internet users (% of population)	51.1	⬆

◆— ADB DMC mean & range   ● Country indicator value   ⬆ SDG Trend

x-axis: 0, 20, 40, 60, 80, 100

ADB = Asian Development Bank, DMC = developing member country, GDP = gross domestic product, SDG = Sustainable Development Goal, SE4All = sustainable energy for all.

Source: ADB analysis based on Asia-Pacific SDG Partnership. 2020. SDG Progress.

B. Planet

Sun power. A woman trained under the Rural Electricians Training Program fixes a rooftop solar panel in Bhutan (photo by Asian Development Bank).

Figure 9: ADB Support for Planet-Related Sustainable Development Goals in 2019

SECTOR-BASED GOALS	%PROJECTS(#)	SELECTED RESULTS OF 2019 COMPLETED OPERATIONS
12 RESPONSIBLE CONSUMPTION AND PRODUCTION	**15%**	• 5,137,000 people benefiting from strengthened environmental sustainability
14 LIFE BELOW WATER	**1%**	• 870 hectares of terrestrial, coastal, and marine areas conserved, restored, and/or enhanced
15 LIFE ON LAND	**1%**	• Nine solutions to conserve, restore, and/or enhance terrestrial, coastal, and marine areas implemented

CROSSCUTTING THEMATIC GOALS

13 CLIMATE ACTION	**62%**	• 3,161,000 people with strengthened climate and disaster resilience • 1,588,000 women and girls with increased resilience to climate change, disasters, and other external shocks • 12,778,000 tCO2e/year total annual greenhouse gas emissions reduction

tCO2e = tons of carbon dioxide equivalent.

Source: Asian Development Bank. 2020. 2019 Development Effectiveness Review: Scorecard and Related Information.

1. Context

Regional progress. Protecting the planet and restoring ecosystems are urgent challenges in a region where growth has often come with a high environmental cost. The region has made limited progress on the environmental SDGs. In 2018, Asia and Pacific DMCs accounted for about half of global greenhouse gas (GHG) emissions, and the region contains almost all of the 100 most polluted cities in the world. These pressures, as well as natural hazards and climate change-related events, such as forest fires in Indonesia to floods in Bangladesh, which afflict millions of people across the region each year, take a major toll on people's health and add to the severe stresses facing the region's ecosystems and biodiversity.

Despite the slowing of economic activity because of measures to contain the COVID-19 pandemic, the overall reduction in GHG emissions is estimated to have been less than 7%, reflecting the need for much more ambitious action on climate change (SDG 13).[19] Pandemic management measures have also led to increased medical waste and use of plastics, and other resource stresses. In 2021, a series of major global summits seeks to focus global attention on addressing these challenging and interlinked issues. Forthcoming summits include the 15th meeting of the Conference of the Parties to the Convention on Biological Diversity, where a focus on biodiversity finance is planned;

and the 26th Conference of the Parties to the UN Framework Convention on Climate Change, where countries will be asked to announce more ambitious Nationally Determined Contributions (NDCs) of climate action. Several countries in the region have already revised their NDCs.

Key features of ADB's approach. ADB's operational priority 3 aims to tackle climate change, build climate and disaster resilience, and enhance environmental sustainability. Key priorities set out in the operational plan include scaling up support to address climate change, disaster risks, and environmental degradation; accelerating low GHG emission development; pursuing a comprehensive approach to building climate and disaster resilience; ensuring environmental sustainability; and increasing the focus on the water–food–energy nexus. All seven Strategy 2030 operational priorities are linked to efforts to promote environmentally sustainable, low-carbon, and climate-resilient development (footnote 11). ADB's safeguards also play a crucial role in managing potential negative environmental effects of development investments.[20] Safeguard implementation and related capacity building within DMCs helps strengthen systems for environmental management and effective management of related trade-offs.

> **The COVID-19 economic crisis is estimated to have reduced GHG emissions by less than 7%, reflecting the need for much more ambitious action on climate change.**

---

[19] J. Tollefson. 2021. COVID curbed carbon emissions in 2020 — but not by much. Nature. 589, 343. Based on estimates from Friedlingstein, et al.2020. Global Carbon Budget 2021. Earth Syst. Sci. Data, 12, 3269–3340.
[20] ADB. Safeguard Policy Statement.

2. Responsible Consumption and Production

Many ADB programs help DMCs access cleaner and smarter technologies that can foster more responsible production. ADB is also incorporating procurement reforms that aim to encourage green procurement practices and life cycle costing for investments, particularly in the infrastructure sectors. Under operational priority 3, ADB seeks to support DMCs to decouple economic growth from environmental degradation and promote a circular economy. For example, ADB is working with Maldives to improve environmental protection and sustainability in the Greater Male region and its surrounding islands through the establishment of a climate- and disaster-resilient solid waste management system. The Greater Male Environmental Improvement and Waste Management Project will install an improved waste collection, transfer, and disposal system, including collection trucks, transfer stations, waste vessels, and with a rehabilitated harbor. Public awareness campaigns to promote reduce, reuse, and recycle behaviors will complement the structural components of the project. The next phase of this project, the Greater Male Waste-to-Energy Project, will set up a waste-to-energy plant on the island, helping the country to avoid toxic smoke, leachate, and GHG emissions from its current unsustainable solid waste management practices. The waste-to-energy treatment process minimizes the land required for waste disposal and produces renewable energy, helping address the critical land and electricity constraints of small island developing states (SIDS) such as Maldives. This program is closely linked to efforts to support healthier ocean ecosystems, mitigate hazards to fisheries, and promote tourism.

Climate finance from ADB's own resources will reach $80 billion cumulatively from 2019 to 2030.

3. Climate Action

Strategy 2030 sets ambitious climate change targets, including that 75% of its operations will support climate change mitigation and adaptation by 2030 and that climate finance from ADB's own resources will reach $80 billion cumulatively from 2019 to 2030. These targets are closely aligned with those of SDG 13 and are enabled by a range of measures and operational frameworks that support climate action across ADB. These include the Climate Change Operational Framework, 2017–2030, support for carbon markets (Box 6), the adoption of mandatory climate risk screening and assessment of projects since 2014, and systems for GHG accounting and measurement for investments in certain sectors.[21]

ADB supports its DMCs' implementation of the NDCs proposed under the Paris Agreement on Climate Change and is helping them develop more ambitious climate action programs to achieve the agreement's overarching goals. It is also working with other MDBs to ensure that its own investments are aligned with the objectives of the Paris Agreement. ADB helps the DMCs access and use finance to support climate change and environmental action, including from multilateral funds such as the Green Climate Fund, the Climate Investment Funds, and the Global Environment Facility.

---

[21] ADB has issued guidelines for estimating the GHG emissions from transport, energy efficiency, and renewable energy projects (ADB. 2017. Guidelines for Estimating Greenhouse Gas Emissions of ADB Projects).

Harvesting energy from the sun. The 73-megawatt Lopburi solar power plant in central Thailand is the largest solar photovoltaic project in the world (photo by Gerhard Joren).

Box 6: ADB's Support for Carbon Markets

The Asian Development Bank (ADB) was among the earliest supporters of carbon markets to encourage greenhouse gas mitigation activities in its developing member countries (DMCs). It has provided technical and capacity building support to enhance DMCs' ability to participate in and take advantage of carbon markets and scale up mitigation actions. The Asia Pacific Carbon Fund, the Future Carbon Fund, and the Japan Fund for the Joint Crediting Mechanism seek to address key barriers to the development of emission reduction projects by providing innovative carbon finance to incentivize investments in climate change mitigation actions that reduce greenhouse gas emissions and deliver development benefits. ADB will continue to adopt a holistic approach by helping DMCs enhance their technical capacity to access carbon finance and meet commitments under their Nationally Determined Contributions, raising ambition over time and supporting sustainable development in the region.

Source: Asian Development Bank.

In the PRC, ADB is supporting the Shandong Green Development Fund, which will pilot an innovative leveraging mechanism to catalyze private, institutional, and commercial capital to support climate-positive infrastructure and business in Shandong Province. The fund will help the Shandong Provincial Government implement its progressive climate policies and invest in climate-positive subprojects. The pipeline of subprojects will be screened against the fund's Green Climate Assessment Guidelines and categorized as exhibiting good practices, providing advanced benefits, or being transformational, depending on the anticipated impacts. Financing terms will be linked to these climate benefits.

In Viet Nam, ADB provided a nonsovereign loan to Da Nhim–Ham Thuan–Da Mi Hydro Power Joint Stock Company for the country's first large-scale installation of floating solar photovoltaic panels. Aligned with Viet Nam's commitments to the UN Framework Convention on Climate Change, the Floating Solar Energy Project helps boost the share of renewable energy in the country's overall energy mix and improves the amount of output from a single source by pairing two clean energy technologies—hydropower and solar.

ADB is also supporting investment in innovative green financing programs in Southeast Asia. The ASEAN Catalytic Green Finance Facility helps governments create bankable green infrastructure projects and enabled the Government of Thailand to issue its maiden sustainability bond series under its Sustainable Financing Framework in August 2020 to access capital markets for a post-COVID-19 green recovery. The Public Debt Management Office of the Ministry of Finance issued

the bond in two fixed rate tranches for a total principal aggregate amount of B50 billion (about $1.6 billion). The sustainability bond is one of the first sovereign bonds issued globally since the COVID-19 pandemic to support the recovery.

The Pacific Disaster Resilience Program fills a financing gap experienced by Pacific DMCs that are hit hard by disasters. It provides the Cook Islands, the Marshall Islands, the Federated States of Micronesia, Palau, Samoa, Solomon Islands, Tonga, and Tuvalu and with a predictable and quick-disbursing source of financing for timely response, recovery, and reconstruction activities, and supports their priority disaster risk management actions. The program also encourages the sharing of experiences between Pacific countries in close alignment with the work of other development partners and guided by the region's own framework for resilient development.

ADB has used policy-based loans to support systemic transitions toward low-carbon development. For example, the Beijing–Tianjin–Hebei Air Quality Improvement–Hebei Policy Reforms Program in the PRC has enabled policy actions to switch from coal to cleaner energy, promote public transport in urban areas, and increase use of biomass for energy in rural areas. The program paved the way for energy and socioeconomic reforms, and investments in improving air quality and public health, including pollution management. ADB's support will contribute to the PRC's commitment to reduce GHG emissions and strengthen its environment regulatory framework and environmental monitoring and enforcement capacity.

4. Life below Water

Under the Action Plan for Healthy Oceans and Sustainable Blue Economies, launched in 2019, ADB will expand financing and technical assistance for ocean health and marine economy projects to $5 billion during 2019–2024. The plan focuses on creating inclusive livelihoods and business opportunities in sustainable tourism and fisheries; protecting and restoring coastal and marine ecosystems and key rivers; reducing land-based sources of marine pollution including plastics, wastewater, and agricultural runoff; and improving the

sustainability of ports and other coastal infrastructure. It includes an oceans financing initiative that aims to create opportunities for the private sector to invest in viable projects that will improve ocean health.

In 2020, ADB made a blue loan to Indorama Ventures Public Company Limited, a Thailand-listed global business that is the largest producer of 100% recyclable polyethylene terephthalate plastics in the world. ADB's financial assistance will help reduce the environmental impact of plastic and promote a circular economy by boosting the capacity of the company's plastic recycling plants in India, Indonesia, the Philippines, and Thailand. This is ADB's first nonsovereign blue loan following the Blue Natural Capital Financing Facility's blue bond guidelines and with an assurance report from DNV GL, an international accredited registrar and classification society. ADB is exploring further blue finance opportunities across the region.

Recognizing that transformational change requires multi-stakeholder action, ADB plays an active role in initiatives such as the Advisory Network to the High Level Panel for a Sustainable Ocean Economy and the Coral Triangle Initiative on Coral Reefs, Fisheries, and Food Security. Partners include the European Investment Bank through the Clean and Sustainable Oceans Partnership, the Nature Conservancy, and WWF.

5. Protecting Terrestrial Ecosystems

ADB helps its DMCs manage their natural resources in a manner that protects, maintains, and improves the productive potential of natural capital. The COVID-19 pandemic has underscored the close connections between humans and the natural world and reinforced the need to invest in nature-based solutions to development challenges. In the PRC, for instance, the Sichuan Ziyang Inclusive Green Development Project will support the municipal government in pursuing a greener development approach. The project will invest in ecological systems and environmental infrastructure, including "eco-dike" flood control embankments to protect against 1-in-50-year flood events, "sponge city" interventions to capture storm water, and wetland area development to improve water quality in Yannan Lake. The project will also transform a landfill site into a green park, create a natural barrier between Ziyang's old residential and industrial areas, and preserve the ecology of hillsides at risk of erosion.

The intervention in Ziyang will be a demonstration project for similar medium-sized cities in the middle and upper reaches of the Yangtze River Economic Belt (YREB), where ADB is taking a programmatic approach to help communities achieve water security and green development and increase their resilience. The YREB program includes a portfolio of lending and nonlending projects on ecological protection and water quality improvement that is consistent with the PRC's YREB Development Plan. The approach of designing project clusters and strengthening institutional coordination across provincial boundaries and geographic scales and sectors provides a model for addressing environmental, social, and economic issues in a more integrated and holistic manner.

Spotlight: Cambodia

Cambodia has made important progress on some dimensions of the 2030 Agenda for Sustainable Development. It has prepared a Cambodia Sustainable Development Goals (SDGs) framework and has reflected it in its National Strategic Development Plan, 2019–2023. Before the onset of the coronavirus disease (COVID-19) pandemic, Cambodia's rapid economic growth and increase in investment enhanced opportunities for SDG financing from public and private sources. Various plans also bolster its SDG agenda, including the Health Strategic Plan, 2016–2020 and the National Strategy for the Development of Statistics, 2018–2023. Cambodia monitors its SDG progress using the Cambodia SDGs framework, the Cambodia SDGs indicator database, and national data sources. The Asian Development Bank (ADB) and the United Nations Development Programme prepared an SDG Country Implementation Snapshot for Cambodia in 2019.

ADB has been supporting Cambodia since 1966 and is the country's largest multilateral development partner. ADB's country partnership strategy for Cambodia, 2019–2023 defines its strategic approach to the delivery of operations and consists of four pillars: competitiveness and economic diversification; human capital; green, sustainable, and inclusive development; and governance.

ADB has supported the decentralization efforts of the National Committee for Sub-National Democratic Development. Under regional technical assistance for Strengthening Institutions for Localizing Agenda 2030 for Sustainable Development, ADB has also organized forums on institutional capacity for SDG localization with United Cities and Local Governments and the National League of Local Councils of Cambodia. These events provide opportunities to strengthen the role of local institutions in SDG planning and implementation.

ADB helped the Ministry of Economy and Finance pilot a skills development fund to foster engagement with industry. ADB's loan for the Skills for Competitiveness Project expands the pilot Skills Development Fund, an innovative model to increase and incentivize industry investments in upskilling and reskilling current workers to develop the workforce of the future.

ADB also provided a sovereign loan for the Cambodia Solar Power Project in 2016 to finance the first utility-scale solar generation with 10 megawatts (MW) capacity in the country. This was followed in 2019 by the National Solar Park Project, a pathbreaking public–private partnership transaction that secured the lowest tariff for solar power generation in Asia with an initial generation capacity of 40 MW. ADB provided transaction advisory services for the National Solar Park public–private partnership project and is providing transaction advisory services for a second phase of the solar park development that will add a further 60 MW of generation capacity. In 2020, ADB approved a loan for the Grid Reinforcement Project to support the expansion of transmission lines and substations, a component to pilot grid-scale battery storage, and further investments in energy efficiency.

ADB has provided about 25% of total external assistance for water supply and sanitation services in Cambodia's urban and rural areas, making it one of the largest supporters of these services. The Third Rural Water Supply and Sanitation Services Sector Development Program is constructing and rehabilitating 2,500 rural water facilities in at least 400 villages across 10 Cambodian provinces, aiming to benefit more than 400,000 people. It also supports the construction of new toilets for individual households, public latrines at schools and health centers, and health promotion through hygiene and sanitation awareness campaigns.

ADB's country partnership strategy for Cambodia, 2019–2023 defines its strategic approach to the delivery of operations and consists of four pillars: competitiveness and economic diversification; human capital; green, sustainable, and inclusive development; and governance.

Progress on Selected Indicators

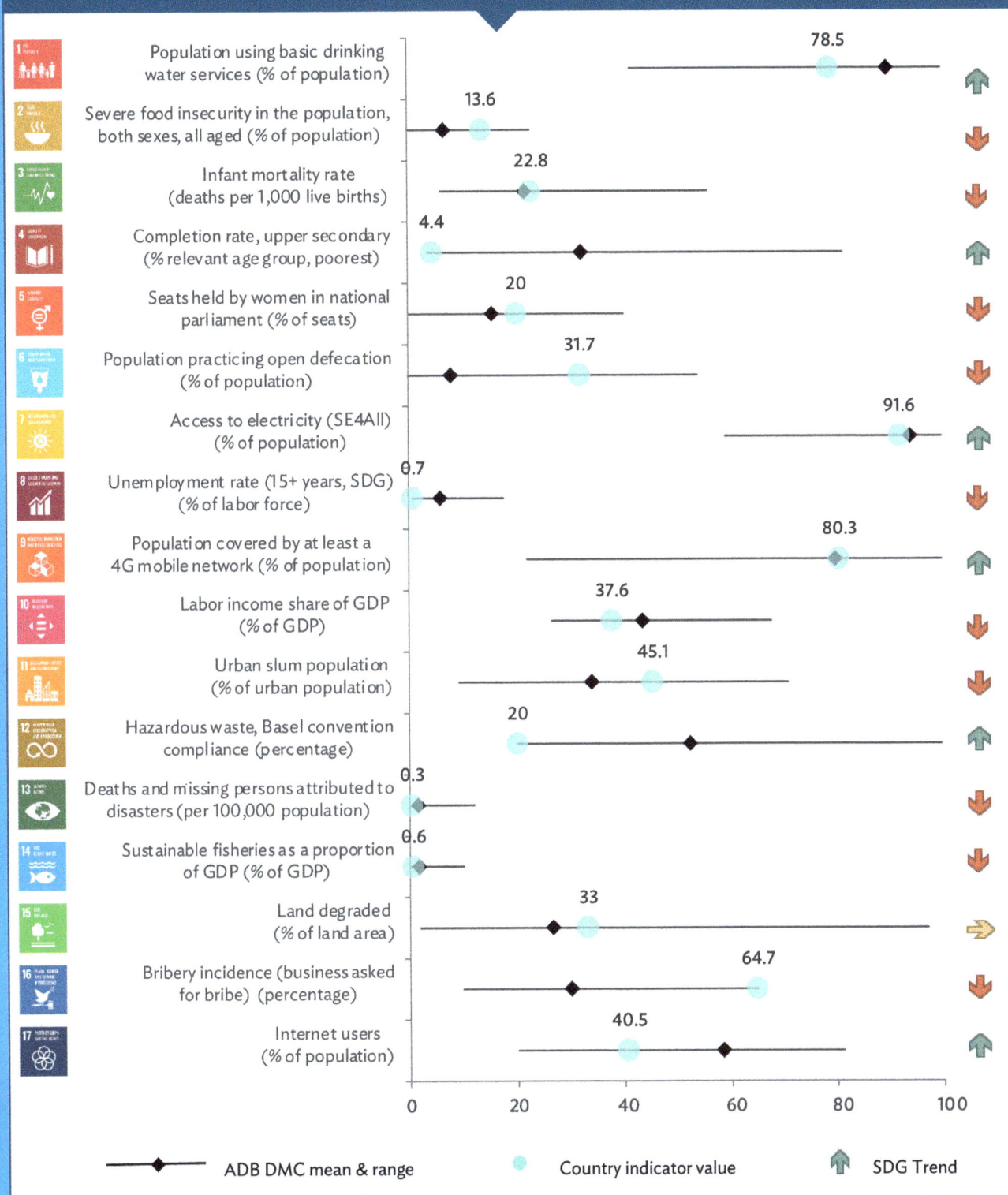

Indicator	Value	SDG Trend
Population using basic drinking water services (% of population)	78.5	↑
Severe food insecurity in the population, both sexes, all aged (% of population)	13.6	↓
Infant mortality rate (deaths per 1,000 live births)	22.8	↓
Completion rate, upper secondary (% relevant age group, poorest)	4.4	↑
Seats held by women in national parliament (% of seats)	20	↓
Population practicing open defecation (% of population)	31.7	↓
Access to electricity (SE4All) (% of population)	91.6	↑
Unemployment rate (15+ years, SDG) (% of labor force)	0.7	↓
Population covered by at least a 4G mobile network (% of population)	80.3	↑
Labor income share of GDP (% of GDP)	37.6	↓
Urban slum population (% of urban population)	45.1	↓
Hazardous waste, Basel convention compliance (percentage)	20	↑
Deaths and missing persons attributed to disasters (per 100,000 population)	0.3	↓
Sustainable fisheries as a proportion of GDP (% of GDP)	0.6	↓
Land degraded (% of land area)	33	⇒
Bribery incidence (business asked for bribe) (percentage)	64.7	↓
Internet users (% of population)	40.5	↑

x-axis: 0   20   40   60   80   100

◆—— ADB DMC mean & range   ● Country indicator value   ⬆ SDG Trend

ADB = Asian Development Bank, DMC = developing member country, GDP = gross domestic product, SDG = Sustainable Development Goal, SE4All = sustainable energy for all.

Source: ADB analysis based on Asia-Pacific SDG Partnership. 2020. SDG Progress.

A day at the bank. Banco Nacional de Comércio de Timor-Les[te] tellers attend to clients at their main bank branch in Dili, the capi[tal] of the country (photo by Luis Ascu[...]).

SECTOR-BASED GOALS	%PROJECTS(#)	SELECTED RESULTS OF 2019 COMPLETED OPERATIONS
8 DECENT WORK AND ECONOMIC GROWTH	**16%**	• 313,000 jobs generated • Two enhanced labor policies or standards implemented • Four new financial products and services made available to the poor and vulnerable
16 PEACE AND JUSTICE STRONG INSTITUTIONS	**5%**	• 1,700 entities with improved management functions and financial stability

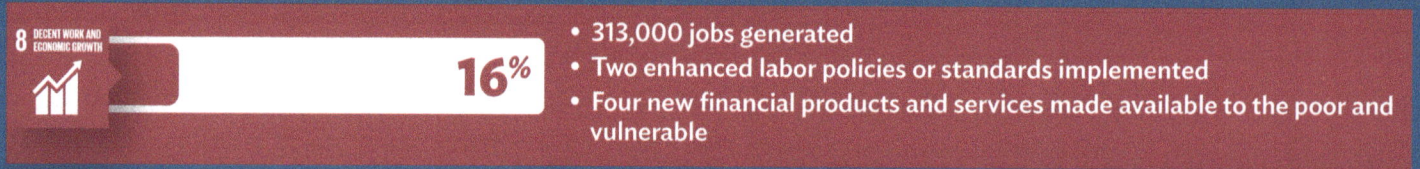

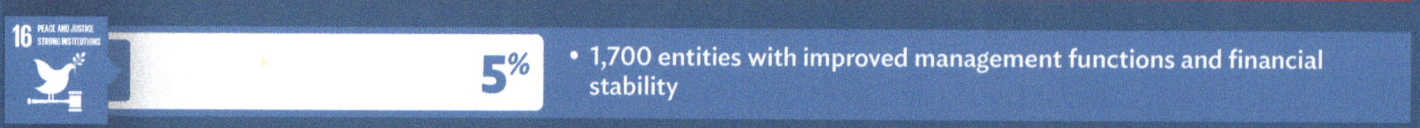

CROSSCUTTING THEMATIC GOALS

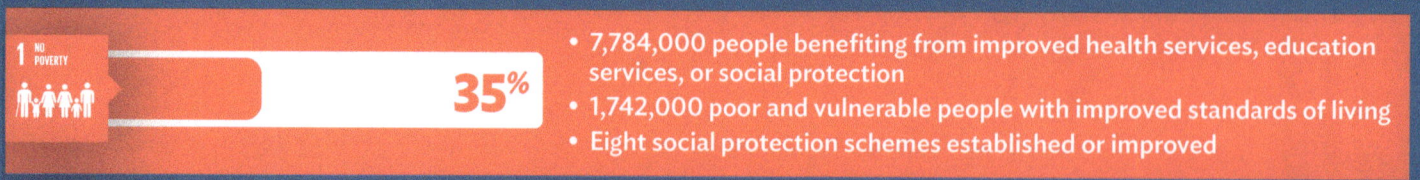

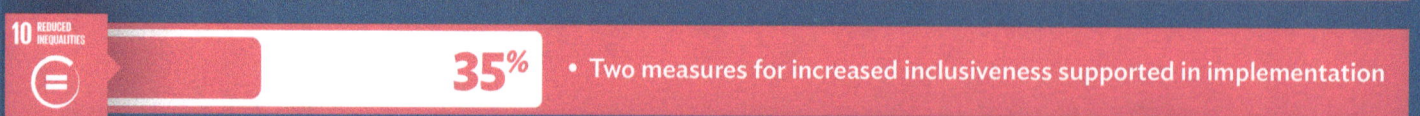

1 NO POVERTY	**35%**	• 7,784,000 people benefiting from improved health services, education services, or social protection • 1,742,000 poor and vulnerable people with improved standards of living • Eight social protection schemes established or improved
10 REDUCED INEQUALITIES	**35%**	• Two measures for increased inclusiveness supported in implementation

Source: Asian Development Bank. 2020. 2019 Development Effectiveness Review: Scorecard and Related Information.

1. Context

Regional progress. Rapid economic growth and significant reductions in extreme poverty have been accompanied by inequalities of income and opportunity across the region.[22] Even before the pandemic, more than 1 billion people in Asia had no access to formal financial services.[23] Women were 9% less likely than men to have a bank account in developing economies globally in 2017, and in South Asia this figure was 18%.[24] The average proportion of youth not in education, training, or employment was nearly 20% in 2019. The COVID-19 crisis and measures taken to contain the spread of the virus, such as movement restrictions and business closures, have stalled revenue streams from remittances and tourism receipts and shuttered SMEs, reversing progress made on the SDG 8 agenda of decent work and economic growth.

DMCs' institutional capacity also impacts prosperity. Areas such as governance, project implementation, data management, and domestic resource mobilization all influence the SDG agendas. Tax collection in the region remains some of the lowest globally. In 2016, the central government tax revenues of the developing countries of Asia and the Pacific averaged 16.1% of gross domestic product (GDP).[25] In 2018 these ranged from 11.9% of GDP in Indonesia to 35.4% in Nauru.[26] Countries classified as fragile and conflict-affected situations (FCAS) and small island developing states (SIDS) face particular constraints to poverty reduction and inclusive growth, such as vulnerability to economic shocks and weak public administration, necessitating tailored and context-sensitive assistance.

Key features of ADB's approach. Strategy 2030 envisions a prosperous Asia and the Pacific, while continuing to address extreme poverty. Addressing poverty in all its forms, including income poverty, as envisaged in SDG 1, while reducing inequalities, as set out in SDG 10, are central to ADB operations. Many projects include a focus on vulnerable people, including migrants, and on situations of conflict and fragility. Strategy 2030 also emphasizes the need to strengthen governance and institutional capacity, particularly through improved public sector management and service delivery, and seeks to support more accountable and responsive institutions that manage economies effectively to promote growth and prosperity for all.

Operational priority 6 recognizes the inherent links between the quality of governance and the quality of growth in ADB's DMCs, and the central role of enhancing institutional capacity and governance in the region to achieve the SDGs. ADB operations are shaped by its governance and anticorruption policies and associated action plans, and its capacity development framework, which aims to improve the mainstreaming of capacity development principles and practices. Consistent with this approach, ADB's efforts have increasingly been focused on promoting corruption-free delivery of public services, the implementation of anticorruption measures, and strengthening anti-money-laundering and tax integrity standards in the DMCs. ADB also works with civil society and citizen networks to ensure accountability, transparency, and inclusion, and promotes programming approaches that are participatory and gender and socially inclusive. Tailored approaches to addressing these themes seek to respond to the heterogenous needs and circumstances of the DMCs.

---

[22] OECD. 2019. Society at a Glance: Asia/Pacific 2019. The Gini coefficient of income distribution ranges from 0 (perfect equality of incomes) to 1 (perfect inequality).
[23] World Bank. 2018. Financial Inclusion for Asia's Unbanked.
[24] World Bank. 2017. The Global Findex Database 2017.
[25] ESCAP, ADB, and UNDP. 2019. Accelerating Progress: An Empowered, Inclusive and Equal Asia and the Pacific.
[26] OECD. 2018. Revenue Statistics in Asian and Pacific Economies 2020.

2. Addressing Remaining Poverty and Reducing Inequalities

ADB's investments address poverty and inequality in diverse ways, particularly through operational priorities 1 and 2. Initial poverty and social analyses set out the ways in which projects will benefit the poor and provide social development impacts. Through these analyses, which are required for all investment projects, potential social issues are addressed during project preparation to ensure that project design maximizes social benefits and avoids or minimizes social risks, particularly for vulnerable and marginalized groups. ADB also considers the needs of migrant workers, who are often especially vulnerable, and has developed targeted programs to address them (Box 7).

ADB's project classification system captures projects that seek to directly target poverty. A core and continued area of focus is on strengthening social protection systems in the region to meet the needs of the poor and marginalized groups. The technical assistance program, Strategies for Financing Social Protection to Achieve Sustainable Development Goals in Developing Member Countries, helps DMCs fulfill the social protection agenda of the SDGs. Studies in selected countries provide evidence for the need for greater investments in social protection systems, and support policy dialogue and reform to this end.[27]

Box 7: Leaving No One Behind: Migrants

Tajikistan's narrow economic base and heavy dependence on remittances by labor migrants make it vulnerable to external shocks. The Asian Development Bank (ADB) estimates that remittances to Tajikistan will have shrunk by at least 35% in 2020 because of the combined effects of the coronavirus disease (COVID-19) pandemic, which has affected both domestic and destination labor markets for migrants from the country, and depressed oil prices.

To help unemployed workers and returning migrants acquire skills and find jobs during and after COVID-19, ADB is supporting the Skills and Employability Enhancement Project.

Three new migration service centers will be built and equipped in the cities of Bokhtar, Khujand, and Vose as one-stop centers for departing and returning migrants. The centers will offer migration orientation programs, and training in language and entry-level preemployment skills to help migrants find better jobs and safer living conditions in the destination countries. The centers will also provide financial literacy training for secure remittance transmission and information and communication technology training for easier access to social welfare information.

The project will establish and equip three new model job centers in the capital, Dushanbe, for tourism; in Rogun for energy; and in Dangara for agriculture. They will provide enhanced skills training, childcare centers, a pilot stipend program for female job seekers, a pilot program for new and more focused soft skills training, job counseling services to match interests and skills to potential jobs, and information and communication technology skills training.

Source: Asian Development Bank.

---

[27] For example, ADB's 2018 report, Asia's Fiscal Challenge: Financing the Social Protection Agenda of the Sustainable Development Goals, provides an analysis of the fiscal requirements to achieve the social protection agenda of the SDGs in Mongolia, Myanmar, and Timor-Leste, and suggests options to address financing gaps in ADB DMCs.

In the Philippines, ADB has been supporting the Pantawid Pamilyang Pilipino Program (4Ps) for a decade. Under the 4Ps, poor households receive cash payments as long as the children meet school attendance targets and have regular health checkups, women avail of pre- and post-natal care, and the parents participate in family development sessions. The Expanded Social Assistance Project is financing a portion of the program's conditional cash transfers to help families maintain the health and educational gains their children achieved under 4Ps. ADB's financial support allows the government to boost its social investment in Filipinos to break the intergenerational cycle of poverty. Technical assistance will be provided to improve the delivery systems for conditional cash transfers and help the Department of Social Welfare and Development institute information technology reforms to improve compliance verification, payroll, and grievance redress systems. It will also strengthen links with complementary social programs, improve the department's project management and evaluation capacity, and help 4Ps households in selected sites to graduate out of poverty with the aid of sustainable livelihood assistance.

The efficiency and impact of the Expanded Social Assistance Project will be enhanced by the Inclusive Finance Development Program, a policy-based loan that will support the implementation of the Philippine national identification system—a necessary starting point for accelerating financial inclusion and an essential tool for effective poverty targeting and provision of social assistance and other government services. The program aims to strengthen the institutional and policy environment for financial services, invest in support networks and infrastructure such as the national retail payment system, and improve the abilities of financial institutions to offer financial products through the application of new technologies. Other areas of support cover agriculture finance, financial literacy, microinsurance, and crop insurance. Following the adoption of a legal and regulatory framework for Islamic finance, this type of financial service will be increased through awareness-raising and capacity development activities for financial institutions. These measures can support inclusion for a large segment of the population, particularly in the conflict-affected areas of Mindanao.

Community-based development can be an effective tool to bring local communities to the forefront of poverty reduction and development efforts by allowing them to identify, design, and implement solutions that address their needs. In Myanmar, for example, ADB has been supporting the Resilient Community Development Project, which aims to develop climate-resilient and market-oriented infrastructure and livelihoods in 2,942 villages in 17 poor townships. Emphasizing local community participation and women's engagement, the project will help identify, develop, and fund 3,000 climate- and disaster-resilient community infrastructure subprojects, including village access or farm roads, small bridges, water supply, electric grid connection, and multipurpose centers. The project will also include a disaster contingency feature to allow for the immediate disbursement of funds for the reconstruction of damaged infrastructure and the recovery of livelihoods in case a disaster affects an entire township.

ADB supports community-based development that brings local communities to the forefront of poverty reduction efforts by allowing them to identify, design, and implement projects.

Spotlight: Nepal

The Government of Nepal's National Planning Commission has established a three-tiered coordination mechanism for the Sustainable Development Goals (SDGs) and has taken steps to integrate the SDGs into national planning frameworks. An SDG coordination committee has been formed that has developed an SDG status, road map, needs assessment, costing, and financing strategy and is taking initial steps to reflect the SDGs in its federal budget planning processes. The Asian Development Bank (ADB) is supporting these efforts in partnership with the United Nations Development Programme, and they jointly prepared an SDG Country Implementation Snapshot for Nepal in 2019. Nepal monitors SDG progress using data from the National Planning Commission's 2017 SDG baseline survey, the National Review of the SDGs in June 2020, and other socioeconomic censuses and surveys. It is developing an SDG data platform and plans to conduct its next population census in 2021, which will provide further disaggregated socioeconomic data.

ADB's country partnership strategy for Nepal, 2020–2024 focuses on three objectives: providing infrastructure for private sector-led growth, improving access to devolved services, and increasing environmental sustainability and resilience. Particular priorities are hydropower and renewable energy, road and air transport infrastructure, and logistics and trade connectivity.

ADB is working with the Nepal Water and Energy Development Company Private Limited on the Upper Trishuli-1 Hydropower Project to enhance Nepal's energy security by helping capitalize on its renewable hydropower potential and reduce electricity imports. Once operational, the 216-megawatt hydropower plant and 1.2 kilometers of transmission lines will generate and dispatch 1,282 gigawatts of clean electricity annually to the national grid, avoiding greenhouse gas emissions equal to 446,000 tons of carbon dioxide per year.

ADB is supporting the government's efforts to improve services for Nepal's rapidly growing urban population by investing in climate-resilient and accessible water supply and sanitation infrastructure. The Urban Water Supply and Sanitation (Sector) Project aims to install or rehabilitate 1,600 kilometers of water supply pipes and 15 water treatment plants, each with a capacity of about 600,000 liters a day. About 66,000 households will be connected to piped water supply, with subsidized connections for 8,000 poor and 2,000 vulnerable households. Women will benefit from spending less time collecting and managing water, gaining opportunities for work

and training, and participating in project consultations and in the 20 water users' and sanitation committees that will be set up. The emerging results of these projects are brought to life in ADB's interactive Results Reality website.

A policy-based loan in 2021 will support reforms to strengthen devolved service delivery through enhanced provincial and local public financial management services, including by expanding electronic government procurement and capacity building initiatives. ADB is also supporting Nepal to improve access, equity, and the quality of education through results-based lending. Focusing on secondary education, the key features of the Supporting School Sector Development Plan include deployment of trained subject teachers, a pro-poor scholarship scheme, improved examinations, pilot testing of the model school program, and improved school governance.

A technical assistance program approved in late 2020 will provide Knowledge Solutions and Institutional Strengthening for Sustainable Development for Nepal. The program will focus on analytical and diagnostic studies to inform strategies, plans, policies, institutional strengthening, and capacity development of government agencies. It will enable ADB to respond to needs arising from the coronavirus disease (COVID-19) pandemic and other emerging challenges through the development of knowledge products, events, capacity building in policy-making, and training programs for government officials.

ADB and development partners are supporting SDG implementation in Nepal, including by extending access to basic services such as clean drinking water.

Progress on Selected Indicators

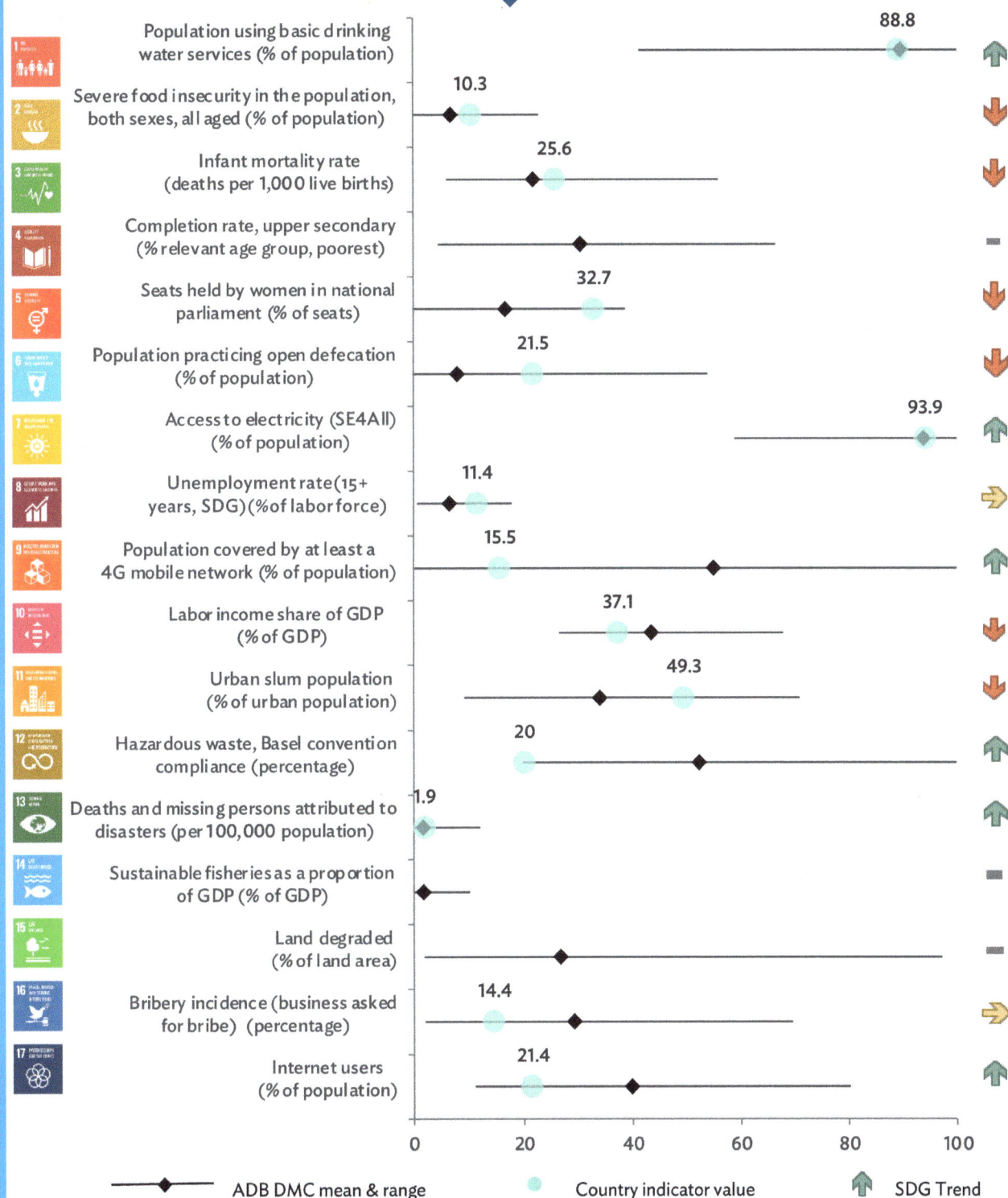

Indicator	Value	SDG Trend
Population using basic drinking water services (% of population)	88.8	↑
Severe food insecurity in the population, both sexes, all aged (% of population)	10.3	↓
Infant mortality rate (deaths per 1,000 live births)	25.6	↓
Completion rate, upper secondary (% relevant age group, poorest)		—
Seats held by women in national parliament (% of seats)	32.7	↓
Population practicing open defecation (% of population)	21.5	↓
Access to electricity (SE4All) (% of population)	93.9	↑
Unemployment rate (15+ years, SDG) (% of labor force)	11.4	⇒
Population covered by at least a 4G mobile network (% of population)	15.5	↑
Labor income share of GDP (% of GDP)	37.1	↓
Urban slum population (% of urban population)	49.3	↓
Hazardous waste, Basel convention compliance (percentage)	20	↑
Deaths and missing persons attributed to disasters (per 100,000 population)	1.9	↑
Sustainable fisheries as a proportion of GDP (% of GDP)		—
Land degraded (% of land area)		—
Bribery incidence (business asked for bribe) (percentage)	14.4	⇒
Internet users (% of population)	21.4	↑

Scale: 0 — 20 — 40 — 60 — 80 — 100

◆——— ADB DMC mean & range   ● Country indicator value   ⬆ SDG Trend

ADB = Asian Development Bank, DMC = developing member country, GDP = gross domestic product, SDG = Sustainable Development Goal, SE4All = sustainable energy for all.

Source: ADB analysis based on Asia-Pacific SDG Partnership. 2020. SDG Progress.

3. Financial Inclusion

Through policy-based loans and programs to promote innovative financial inclusion, ADB is helping the governments of Indonesia and the Philippines build a more inclusive financial services sector as part of these countries' efforts to reduce poverty and inequality and support long-term sustainable development.

Technology can be harnessed to enhance financial inclusion, broaden access to financial services by capitalizing on technological advances, and mitigate the economic shock of COVID-19. ADB is making a range of investments in financial technology to this end. For example, it supported an artificial intelligence-enabled credit score system under the Mekong Business Initiative that helped more than 8,000 SMEs in the Greater Mekong Subregion obtain credit. An ADB-supported cloud-based banking app for Cantilan Bank Inc. in the Philippines and finance sector reforms through the Financial Market Development and Inclusion Program (Subprogram 3) to launch branchless banking in Indonesia have also helped advance financial inclusion.

Job creation is a core priority for ADB, with an emphasis on skills for rapidly changing economies.

4. Promoting Decent Jobs and Economic Growth

Job creation is a core focus of several of ADB's operational priorities, particularly operational priority 1, which includes an emphasis on skills and competencies development to increase the employability of young people. For example, the Chongqing Innovation and Human Capital Development Project in the PRC will build the capacity of higher education institutions to develop courses that focus on emerging engineering and technology fields that contribute to green industrial transformation, such as smart agriculture, logistics, and manufacturing; transportation using alternative energy sources; and reducing industrial pollution and workplace-related accidents. Such efforts will help people in Chongqing municipality gain industry-relevant and innovation-oriented skills and capacities for employment.

Recognizing the critical role of entrepreneurship in boosting prosperity in its DMCs, ADB provides access to finance to help micro, small, and medium-sized enterprises. In Bangladesh, an ADB loan is promoting microenterprise development through a credit line to the Palli Karma Sahayak Foundation (PKSF), a development finance organization, and its partner microfinance institutions. PKSF is an important funding source for small and medium-sized microfinance institutions, but at current funding levels, PKSF and its partner organizations can meet only part of their members' demand. The Microenterprise Development Project will help fill the funding gap. PKSF will onlend the ADB loan to partner organizations to sub-lend to about 40,000 microenterprises, 70% of which are owned or run by women. By providing cost-efficient and reliable access to finance, the project will greatly reduce the cost of funding for beneficiaries and promote the efficient allocation of finance, yielding a higher rate of return from the beneficiaries' microenterprise investments.

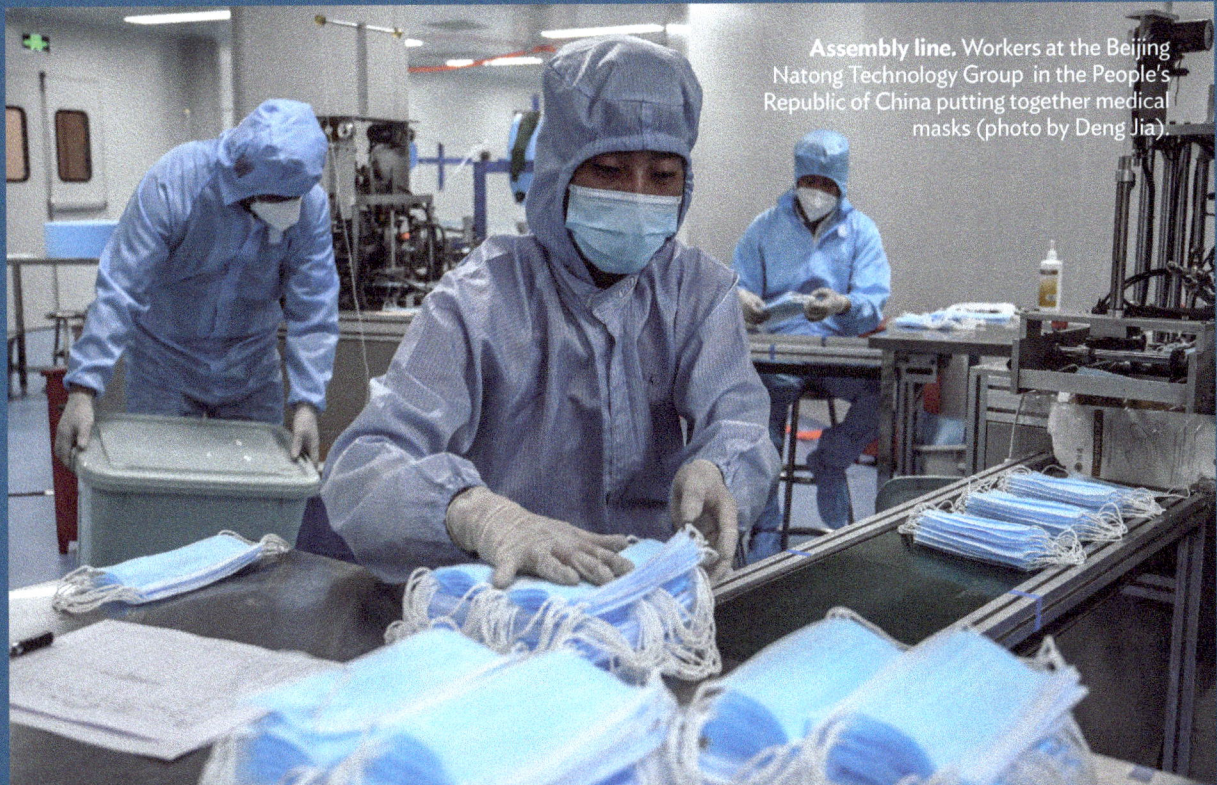

Assembly line. Workers at the Beijing Natong Technology Group in the People's Republic of China putting together medical masks (photo by Deng Jia).

Box 8: Supporting Supply Chain Connectivity amid a Pandemic

The Asian Development Bank (ADB) has brought public and private parties together to help address the impact of the coronavirus disease (COVID-19) pandemic. For example, ADB's Trade and Supply Chain Finance Program partnered with Australian Aid to support the Supply Chain Maps for Pandemic-Fighting Products initiative to map, end-to-end, the entire supply chain for critical pandemic-fighting goods, from ventilators to personal protective equipment, to ensure companies encountered no bottlenecks as they ramped up supply at the height of the outbreak. This was followed by a partnership with HSBC to support up to $1.2 billion a year in trade by companies in Asia and the Pacific that produce goods crucial to combat the pandemic.

Source: Asian Development Bank.

ADB also supports SMEs through its Trade and Supply Chain Finance Program, which fills market gaps for trade financing by providing guarantees and loans to banks. The program works with more than 240 banks in 21 countries to provide companies with the financial support they need to engage in import and export activities in Asia's most challenging markets. In addition to closing gaps through transactions, the program's initiatives include twinning between banks to augment trade finance capacity, creating digital standards for fintech to increase efficiency and strengthen support for SMEs, and promoting greater participation by women in finance. The program has also supported COVID-19 pandemic response measures in ADB DMCs (Box 8). Closing trade finance gaps can promote progress on the SDGs, particularly by contributing to economic growth and poverty reduction, and the economic empowerment of women.[28]

---

28   ADB. 2019. Trade Finance: 2019 Trade Finance Gaps, Growth, and Jobs Survey.

5. Strengthening Governance and Institutional Capacity while Promoting Peace

ADB works to help DMCs build effective, transparent, and accountable institutions, and optimize their fiscal spending to improve the quality and efficiency of public service delivery. ADB's engagement in governance from the national to the local level is a core area of long-standing engagement for ADB and a pillar of ADB's operational priority 6 on strengthening governance and institutional capacity. ADB has invested in building the capacity of subnational entities to provide basic services and has helped support fiscal and service delivery decentralization. COVID-19 has further underscored the role that subnational government plays in supporting sustainable development, as well as the critical role of effective civil society and private sector engagement at all levels of government.

ADB's Office of the General Counsel also supports a range of technical assistance programs that seek to build legal and regulatory capacity among DMCs on critical issues related to SDG implementation, including laws relating to the natural environment, climate change, and the business environment. Examples include technical assistance for Strengthening the Capacity for Environmental and Climate Change Laws in Asia and the Pacific, Enabling a Conducive Environment for the Digital Economy, Developing Judicial Capacity for Adjudicating Climate Change and Sustainable Development Issues, and Strengthening the Efficiency of the Justice Sector with Focus on Commercial Law, Investment, and Contract Enforcement.

In the Lao People's Democratic Republic (Lao PDR), ADB has been a long-term supporter of public financial management reforms. The Strengthening Public Finance Management Program (Subprogram 1) has helped the Lao PDR enhance its public debt management, reform tax administration, improve medium-term fiscal planning and budgeting, and boost governance and budget credibility. This policy-based loan has sought to advance the government's reform agenda and budgeting processes to channel public resources toward the realization of the Lao PDR's Eighth Five-Year National Socio-Economic Development Plan, 2016–2020, which lays a strong foundation for achieving the 2030 Agenda for Sustainable Development.

Similarly, the ADB-supported Building Macroeconomic Resilience Program in Tonga promotes government reforms that will strengthen Tonga's long-term growth prospects and capacity to respond to external shocks. A focus on more efficient customs administration and indirect tax collection to enhance domestic revenue mobilization, and the implementation of a fair and affordable public service remuneration system linked to good performance, will improve the government's fiscal position. Other policy actions include financial management improvements, public enterprise governance reforms, and a streamlined foreign investment registration process. The program also supports the implementation of a private sector development strategy.

ADB also recognizes the special needs of FCAS countries and SIDS in Asia and the Pacific and is developing differentiated and tailored approaches to address their needs and help build their resilience. For example, in Afghanistan and Myanmar, where conflict and insecurity are among the main drivers of fragility, the required context-specific approaches differ from those needed for the seven countries ADB classifies as FCAS and SIDS (Kiribati, the Marshall Islands, the Federated States of Micronesia, Nauru, Papua New Guinea, Solomon Islands, and Tuvalu), where fragility is the result of small size and population, geographic

ADB works to help DMCs build effective, transparent, and accountable institutions, and optimize their fiscal spending to improve the quality and efficiency of public service delivery.

isolation, and disproportionate threats from climate change and natural hazards. In collaboration with other development partners and civil society organizations, ADB continues to strengthen its human resources and staff field presence in these settings; build resilience; and support institutional strengthening and governance reforms, essential infrastructure and social services, targeted social assistance, and private sector operations. For instance, ADB established the Afghanistan Infrastructure Trust Fund to respond to the Government of Afghanistan's need for a dedicated financing mechanism to support infrastructure development in the country. The fund is a multi-donor platform for bilateral, multilateral, and individual contributors to invest in high-priority infrastructure projects that foster the country's economic growth and improve the livelihoods of the Afghan people.

6. Regional Cooperation for Shared Prosperity

Many dimensions of SDG attainment are transboundary in nature. Regional cooperation is therefore crucial. ADB's regional cooperation and integration programs are often anchored in the development of economic corridors, which combine physical investments, such as infrastructure, with support for policies, planning, and regulations for improved connectivity and cross-border trade to promote shared prosperity.

This comprehensive approach to regional cooperation is exemplified by the development of the Almaty–Bishkek Economic Corridor under the Central Asia Regional Economic Cooperation (CAREC) Program. ADB financed the road transport infrastructure improvements to strengthen connectivity between the two economic centers of Kazakhstan and the Kyrgyz Republic, and it continues to provide support for the transformation of the area into a single space where exchange of ideas and movement of goods and people is fast, easy, and barrier free. ADB's technical assistance for Almaty–Bishkek Economic Corridor Support aims to identify and prepare investment projects along the corridor, particularly in agriculture and tourism; promote private sector investment; and support cooperation between the two governments to develop a common regulatory environment that is consistent with agreements under the Eurasian Economic Union.

In addition, CAREC identifies opportunities for cooperation and integration through its five operational clusters: economic and financial stability; trade, tourism, and economic corridors; infrastructure and economic connectivity; agriculture and water; and human development—all of which contribute to the SDGs. The CAREC 2030 Strategic Framework's cluster approach allows for links and synergies among the various clusters and sectors, such as between water, food, and energy security in the region, and can support interventions that balance the region's needs across these sectors.

ADB collaborates with its DMCs to leverage regional cooperation and integration platforms to provide regional public goods. For example, in the Greater Mekong Subregion, ADB has facilitated cross-border cooperation to maximize synergies between the health systems of Cambodia, the Lao PDR, Myanmar, and Viet Nam and consolidate health security as a regional public good. The Greater Mekong Subregion Health Security Project has strengthened surveillance and outbreak response, laboratory quality and biosafety, and health services access in the subregion. The flexibility and adaptability of the project allowed its funds to be quickly deployed to respond to COVID-19, supporting early efforts to minimize the health impacts of the pandemic in the subregion.

Spotlight: Kazakhstan

The Asian Development Bank (ADB) has worked closely with development partners in Kazakhstan, particularly the United Nations system, to help the country establish institutional arrangements to implement the Sustainable Development Goals (SDGs) and support their localization and acceleration.

ADB operations are implemented under the country partnership strategy for Kazakhstan, 2017–2021, which has three pillars: economic diversification, inclusive development, and sustainable growth. It focuses on helping lessen Kazakhstan's dependence on commodity exports, improve agricultural productivity, reduce inequalities, generate employment, develop renewable energy sources, and address vulnerabilities associated with climate change.

In 2019, ADB and United Nations Development Programme helped the country prepare its first voluntary national review to nationalize and localize the SDGs. Subsequently, they also partnered to perform a rapid integrated assessment of national budgets and a development finance assessment, aimed at further supporting SDG acceleration. The Committee on Statistics of the Ministry of National Economy monitors the SDGs using its SDG Indicator System in the National SDG Platform, comprising global and national (alternative and additional) indicators.

ADB also provided technical assistance to create a development partners' coordination council. The council will serve as a platform for coordination with the government to address gaps in knowledge and investment to achieve the SDGs.

In January 2020, ADB approved the provision of knowledge and support technical assistance for Promoting Digital Technologies for Sustainable Development. This assistance proved particularly timely and relevant during the coronavirus disease (COVID-19) pandemic as digital systems have become lifelines for social and economic systems.

Under the technical assistance for the Establishment of the Kazakhstan Knowledge Center on Integrated Water Resources Management, ADB is helping introduce satellite remote sensing and drones to prepare detailed water accounting systems of the country's river basins that will improve the use of irrigation and enhance agriculture productivity. The project is a collaboration between ADB; the Committee for Water Resources of the Ministry of Ecology, Natural Resources and Geology; and the Kazakhstan Space Agency under the Ministry of Digital Development, Defense and Aerospace Industry.

ADB is also supporting a financial intermediation loan through the Housing Construction and Savings Bank of Kazakhstan, under which only female borrowers are eligible to receive housing loans.

ADB has worked closely with development partners to help Kazakhstan coordinate, report on, and implement the SDGs.

Progress on Selected Indicators

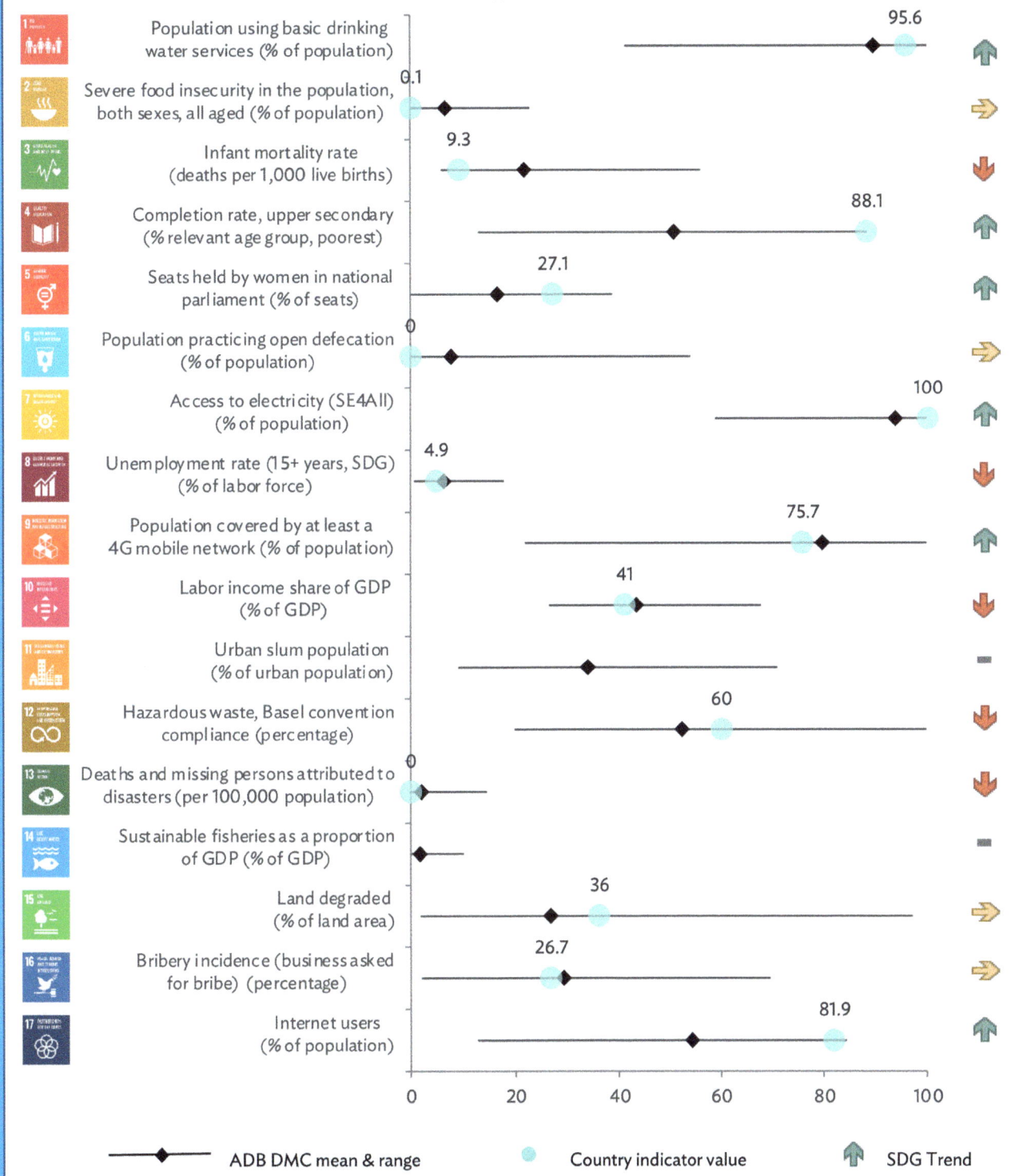

Indicator	Value	ADB DMC mean & range	SDG Trend
Population using basic drinking water services (% of population)	95.6		↑
Severe food insecurity in the population, both sexes, all aged (% of population)	0.1		⇒
Infant mortality rate (deaths per 1,000 live births)	9.3		↓
Completion rate, upper secondary (% relevant age group, poorest)	88.1		↑
Seats held by women in national parliament (% of seats)	27.1		↑
Population practicing open defecation (% of population)	0		⇒
Access to electricity (SE4All) (% of population)	100		↑
Unemployment rate (15+ years, SDG) (% of labor force)	4.9		↓
Population covered by at least a 4G mobile network (% of population)	75.7		↑
Labor income share of GDP (% of GDP)	41		↓
Urban slum population (% of urban population)			–
Hazardous waste, Basel convention compliance (percentage)	60		↓
Deaths and missing persons attributed to disasters (per 100,000 population)	0		↓
Sustainable fisheries as a proportion of GDP (% of GDP)			–
Land degraded (% of land area)	36		⇒
Bribery incidence (business asked for bribe) (percentage)	26.7		⇒
Internet users (% of population)	81.9		↑

◆—— ADB DMC mean & range   ● Country indicator value   ⬆ SDG Trend

ADB = Asian Development Bank, DMC = developing member country, GDP = gross domestic product, SDG = Sustainable Development Goal, SE4All = sustainable energy for all.

Source: ADB analysis based on Asia-Pacific SDG Partnership. 2020. SDG Progress.

D. Sustainable Infrastructure

Charging up. An environmentally-friendlier hybrid bus at a charging station in Peshawar, Pakistan (photo by Rahim Mirza).

Figure 11: ADB Support for Sustainable Infrastructure-Related Sustainable Development Goals in 2019

CROSSCUTTING THEMATIC GOALS	%PROJECTS(#)	SELECTED RESULTS OF 2019 COMPLETED OPERATIONS
6 CLEAN WATER AND SANITATION	15%	• 720 infrastructure assets established or improved
7 AFFORDABLE AND CLEAN ENERGY	17%	• 75,000 MW renewable energy capacity installed
9 INDUSTRY, INNOVATION AND INFRASTRUCTURE	29%	• 18 low-carbon infrastructure assets established or improved • Six new and existing infrastructure assets made climate and disaster- resilient • Six transport and ICT connectivity assets established or improved

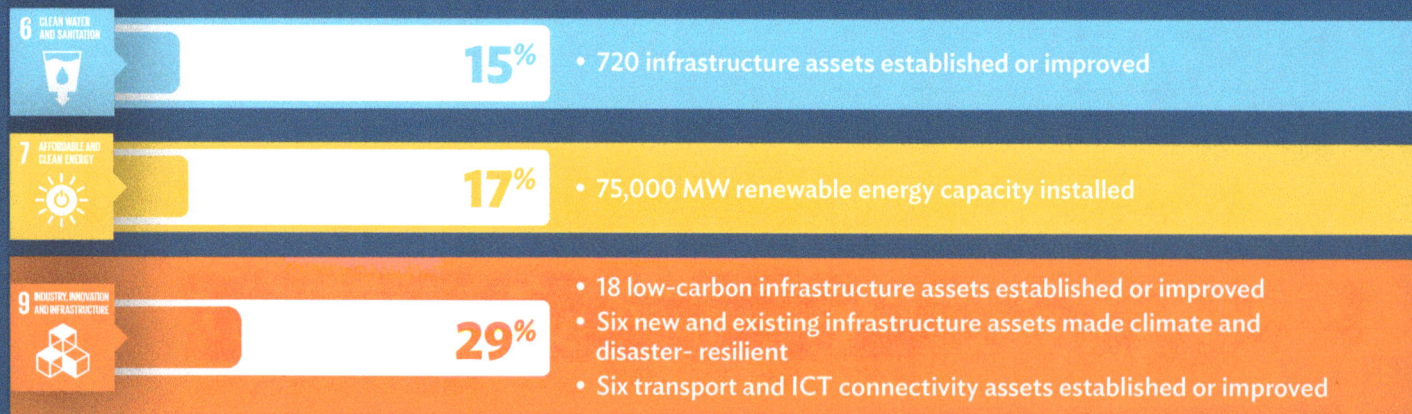

ICT = information and communication technology, MW = megawatt.

Source: Asian Development Bank. 2020. 2019 Development Effectiveness Review: Scorecard and Related Information.

1. Context

Regional progress. Infrastructure underpins growth in Asia and the Pacific and affects the achievement of all the SDGs. The SDGs aspire to provide clean and affordable energy for all. Access to electricity has increased rapidly in recent years, although progress has been uneven across the region, and installed renewable energy lags agreed SDG targets. Similarly, by 2020 access to basic drinking water increased to nearly 92%, but only about 89% of people in the region have access to drinking water that is safely managed. Access to basic sanitation has also improved, though slowly and with major gaps remaining to be met.[29]

The SDGs also recognize the imperative of ensuring that infrastructure is resilient (and supports resilience), including to promote connectivity, sustainable industry, and innovation. Many other SDGs include infrastructure-focused targets. For example, SDG 3 (Good Health and Well-Being) seeks to address road safety, while SDG 4 (Quality Education) recognizes the need to upgrade education infrastructure. Choices about how to provide infrastructure services also affect prospects for achieving the SDGs related to inclusion, poverty eradication, and the environment. Infrastructure has become a casualty of the pandemic as capital to complete projects and sustainably finance their operation and maintenance has become scarce.

Key features of ADB's approach. Infrastructure investments make up a substantial share of ADB's portfolio and directly support targets under SDGs 6, 7, and 9. Investments in connectivity infrastructure are also a key feature of operational priority 7. Strategy 2030 states that ADB will promote quality infrastructure that is green, resilient, inclusive, and sustainable as a means to deliver on its seven operational priorities and its global commitments to address climate change and strengthen disaster risk management.

All aboard. A mother and her son awaiting departure at a railway station in Bangladesh (photo by M R Hasan).

---

29   ESCAP. 2020. Asia and the Pacific SDG Progress Report 2020.

Box 9: ADB's Green, Resilient, Inclusive, and Sustainable Quality Infrastructure Indicator

The Asian Development Bank (ADB) green, resilient, inclusive, and sustainable (GRIS) quality infrastructure indicator seeks to highlight good practices featured in ADB projects and builds on wider good practice and measurement frameworks including ADB's Sustainable Transport Appraisal Rating framework. Each of the GRIS criteria is aligned with specific Sustainable Development Goal targets and the Group of Twenty Principles for Quality Infrastructure Investment.

RESILIENT
CLIMATE CHANGE, BIODIVERSITY, POLLUTION, AND NATURE-BASED SOLUTIONS
1. Climate change mitigation
2. Pollution and other emissions
3. Resource efficiency
4. Nature-based solutions, and natural
5. capital and ecosystem services

RESILIENT
PHYSICAL AND ECONOMIC
1. Climate risk and vulnerability
2. Resilience and adaptability to natural hazards and other shocks and stresses
3. Maximizing positive impact on sustainable growth and development
4. Data and information for infrastructure service optimization

INCLUSIVE
IN MEETING THE NEEDS OF THE POOREST AND SUPPORTING SOCIAL DEVELOPMENT
1. Gender
2. Accessibility and affordability
3. Job creation and livelihoods
4. Health and safety

SUSTAINABLE
FINANCIAL VIABILITY AND DURABILITY, AND GOVERNANCE ARRANGEMENTS
1. Life cycle cost accounting
2. Operation and maintenance
3. Procurement practices and anticorruption measures
4. Financing strategy

Source: Asian Development Bank.

ADB was one of the first MDBs to develop an indicator to measure and report on the quality of its infrastructure investments with reference to the Group of Twenty Principles for Quality Infrastructure Investment and the SDGs (Box 9). ADB collaborates with other MDBs to support sustainable infrastructure aligned with the SDGs through initiatives including the Global Infrastructure Forum (Box 10), established under the Addis Ababa Action Agenda, and the MDB Infrastructure Cooperation Platform.

ADB has helped create and establish technology platforms such as SOURCE, a joint initiative of the MDBs to support partner countries in developing quality infrastructure projects (Box 11).

Unlocking inclusive, resilient and sustainable technology-driven infrastructure. Representatives from multilateral development banks, United Nations agencies, governments, and businesses at the 2018 Global Infrastructure Forum (photo by Ariel Javellana).

Box 10: The Global Infrastructure Forum

The Global Infrastructure Forum (GIF) was established in 2016 as a follow-up to the Addis Ababa Action Agenda of the Third International Conference on Financing for Development, which recognized the need for development finance institutions to collaborate to steer investment toward sustainable infrastructure if the Sustainable Development Goals were to be realized. The GIF is jointly organized by the multilateral development banks (MDBs) in close partnership with the United Nations.

The Asian Development Bank (ADB) has participated in the GIF since the forum's establishment, when Takehiko Nakao, then President of ADB, spoke about the need to ensure high-quality infrastructure investment, and to combine new and advanced technologies and innovation for climate change and urbanization to make infrastructure investment more sustainable, cleaner, and better for all.

In 2017, ADB's participation looked at ways the MDBs can and are providing advisory services to help countries prepare quality infrastructure projects using tools to enable project pipeline development. In 2018, ADB hosted the GIF on the margins of the World Bank and the International Monetary Fund meetings in Bali, Indonesia, and considered how the MDBs can mobilize greater private finance from commercial lenders and institutional investors such as insurance companies, pension funds, infrastructure funds, and sovereign wealth funds. The 2020 the GIF focused on building a resilient future after the coronavirus disease (COVID-19) pandemic. ADB participated in sessions that explored the role of institutional infrastructure investors during a pandemic and the importance of public–private partnerships.

Source: Asian Development Bank.

Box 11: SOURCE—The Multilateral Platform for Quality Infrastructure

The Asian Development Bank (ADB) supported the development of SOURCE, the multilateral platform for quality infrastructure led and funded by multilateral development banks (MDBs). SOURCE was originated by ADB as the National Infrastructure Information System under a regional technical assistance project in 2009. In 2011 the MDB Working Group on Infrastructure, endorsed by the Group of Twenty Cannes Summit in 2011, decided to transfer management of SOURCE to the Sustainable Infrastructure Foundation and to reinvent it as a multilateral platform supporting systemic changes in the way governments define, develop, and manage their infrastructure projects for traditional procurement and public–private partnerships.

SOURCE provides a comprehensive map of all aspects to consider in the development of quality and sustainable infrastructure, including governance, technical, economic, legal, financial, environmental, and social issues. It also allows targets to be defined to fulfill the Sustainable Development Goals and the Paris Agreement.

ADB is a member of the SOURCE Council, which is composed of representatives from MDBs that are promoting the use of SOURCE by implementing agencies in their member countries. SOURCE has also been used to build technical project development capacity with partner agencies in developing countries.

Source: Asian Development Bank.

2. Clean Water and Sanitation

Improving water and sanitation (SDG 6) has been a long-standing area of focus for ADB's programming. Guided by its Water for All vision for Asia and the Pacific, ADB works to increase investments for improved and sustainable water services in cities and rural communities, with strong links to efforts to support environmentally sustainable development and ambitious climate action.

The Climate Change and Disaster-Resilient Water Resources Sector Project in the Kyrgyz Republic exemplifies ADB's approach. The project will modernize irrigation systems to improve the productivity and disaster resilience of about 20,000 hectares of irrigated land, enhance agricultural and on-farm water management, and improve disaster risk management capacity. It includes pilot testing of a new hydrological monitoring and forecasting system that uses satellite data. To ensure more productive and sustainable long-term outcomes, the project will take an inclusive participatory approach to irrigation subproject implementation, with government and community stakeholders jointly engaged in the planning, design, construction, and subsequent management of the systems.

ADB is also supporting significant water and sanitation improvements. The West Bengal Drinking Water Sector Improvement Project will provide safe drinking water service to about 1.65 million people in three districts affected by arsenic, fluoride, and salinity. It will use a high-technology-based smart water management system to efficiently manage services—a first for large-scale rural water schemes in the country. The Tamil Nadu Urban Flagship Investment Program will develop climate-resilient sewage collection, treatment, and drainage systems in 10 cities, install the country's first solar-powered sewage treatment plant on a pilot basis, and introduce smart water management systems to reduce nonrevenue water and strengthen operational efficiency.

Additional concessional financing is often needed to enable such investments. Funding mobilized from various development partners by the Water Financing Partnership Facility for the implementation of ADB's

water financing program has led to $8.14 billion worth of water investments that are helping more than 117 million people across Asia and the Pacific and supporting vital knowledge work to advance effective approaches.

3. Affordable and Clean Energy

ADB has a long-standing commitment to supporting access to clean energy and is one of the largest lenders for clean energy in the region. In Pakistan, for example, ADB is helping increase access to clean energy and enhance energy security using a results-based approach in Khyber Pakhtunkhwa and Punjab, two of the country's largest provinces. The project will install micro-hydropower plants in off-grid communities in Khyber Pakhtunkhwa, and solar facilities in schools and primary health care facilities in two provinces and at a university in Punjab.

In Sri Lanka, ADB is developing the country's first 100-megawatt wind park. The Wind Power Generation Project will establish procedures to enable the Ceylon Electricity Board—the executing agency for the project—

to act as a wind park developer that can attract private sector investment in future wind power projects using a public–private partnership (PPP) model. These include developing cost benchmarks, conducting competitive bidding for future projects, and managing the flow of intermittent wind energy through the power system.

Similarly, ADB is supporting the largest PPP in Solomon Islands for the financing of the Tina River Hydropower Project to provide clean, reliable, and affordable power and cut the country's heavy reliance on diesel. Once operational, it will supply 68% of the capital's electricity. The project will pilot a benefit-sharing mechanism that will make regular payments to community members in the project area over the 30-year operational period.

ADB supports quality infrastructure that is green, resilient, inclusive, and sustainable.

4. Sustainable Transport

Transport is a critical enabler of development and economic growth in Asia and the Pacific and one of the largest sectors in ADB's portfolio. In line with its Sustainable Transport Initiative, ADB has worked to mainstream environmental and social considerations in its transport operations.

Given the remoteness and unique challenges of Pacific DMCs, ADB has been working to improve the maritime connectivity on which these countries depend. For example, the reconstruction of Aiwo port will make it safer, easier, and cheaper for Nauru to expand its trade ties with other countries. The Sustainable and Climate-Resilient Connectivity Project will transform the largely inoperable

boat harbor into an efficient, reliable, and climate-resilient port. In Samoa, the Enhancing Safety, Security, and Sustainability of Apia Port Project will rehabilitate and upgrade the country's only major seaport to withstand a 100-year storm event and 50-year sea level rise and formulate a multi-hazard disaster preparedness plan. It will also adopt a green port policy and encourage the hiring of more women employees at the Samoa Port Authority.

Investments in roads can support inclusive growth by helping countries connect to economic opportunities and services. Ensuring road safety is a vital element of such initiatives. In Tajikistan, which has a poor record for road safety despite low vehicle ownership, ADB's Central Asia Regional Economic Cooperation Corridors 2, 3, and 5 (Obigarm–Nurobod) Road Project will link Tajikistan to Eurasian and global markets and conduct awareness campaigns to promote road safety. With ADB and CAREC assistance, the Ministry of Transport will develop a road safety strategy and action plan that will provide stakeholders with a reference framework to implement future road safety programs.

Transport and industrial corridor development efforts are important elements. The Visakhapatnam–Chennai Industrial Corridor Development Program, for example, will connect four economic hubs and nine industrial clusters. It will combine related subregional and national infrastructure and policy reform initiatives to support greater ease of doing business and better trade links with South Asia and Southeast Asia. New infrastructure will be built, including state highways and roads, effluent and water treatment plants, drinking water pipes, storm drains, power substations, and power transmission and distribution lines. The program will deliver skills training for 25,000 workers, entrepreneurs, and students, along with an investor promotion plan, to develop businesses along the corridor.

Urban mobility to promote more livable cities is also a vital area of focus. The Mumbai Metro Rail Systems Project is expected to reduce congestion on the suburban rail system and cause a shift in the mode of travel from high greenhouse gas-emitting private cars, trucks, and buses to metro lines that entail lower emissions. The safety of women, children, and disabled people is prioritized through women-only coaches, mobile applications for women's security, separate ticketing counters, vending machines, and a station staffed only by women. The Delhi–Meerut Regional Rapid Transit System Investment Project is designed to provide universal access to safe, reliable urban transport services that promote social inclusion and development, particularly for vulnerable groups, by facilitating mobility and improving accessibility to centers of job opportunities. Station designs will provide universal accessibility, and multimodal integration will ensure seamless connectivity to other transport modes.

ADB is investing in digital transformation and connectivity to foster innovations that enable the SDGs.

5. Digital Infrastructure to Leave No One Behind

ADB is also investing in digital infrastructure to improve connectivity and support sustainable development. Such programs can be particularly vital in the geographically dispersed islands of the Pacific. The North Pacific Regional Connectivity Investment Project supports the development of a fiber-optic cable system linking Palau to the internet cable hub in Guam, while the Samoa Submarine Cable Project links Samoa to Fiji's international submarine cable network. The Improving Internet Connectivity for Micronesia Project complements the two information and communication technology interventions, helping to install a submarine cable connection between Kiritimati Island, Kiribati, and a proposed transpacific cable system connecting Australia and Hawaii, while financing Nauru's share of the East Micronesia Cable System. Access to fast internet services that are affordable and accessible is also helping Kiribati and Palau improve their delivery of health and education services, and supporting e-government.

In 2019, ADB signed a private sector financing agreement with Kacific Broadband Satellites International Limited, a Singapore-based satellite operator, for the Asia-Pacific Remote Broadband Internet Satellite Project which supports the construction, launch, and operation of Kacific1, a geostationary earth orbit, high-throughput communications satellite. This can reach remote areas that would otherwise remain isolated and lacking in crucial services that can improve livelihoods and incomes.

ADB helps its DMCs leverage digital technologies to improve public service delivery. In India, the West Bengal Public Finance Management Reforms Program builds on past policy-based programs by improving operational efficiencies and resource planning and management, and taking a whole-of-government approach to public financial management through the integration of state financial and information systems. This will strengthen the delivery of public services and generate fiscal savings that help the state of West Bengal augment growth-enhancing development financing. The program supports the national government's overarching development objective of making public services more accessible through interoperable e-government platforms.

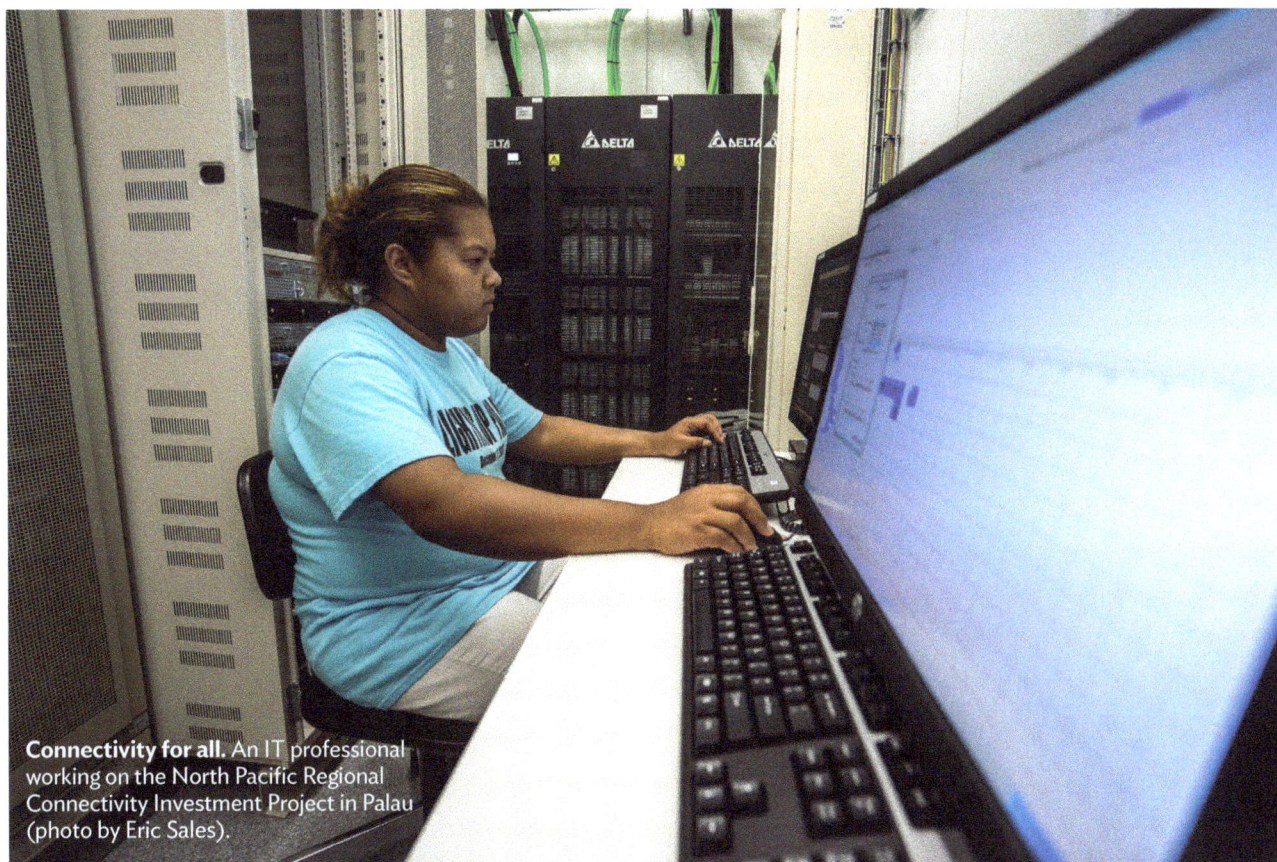

Connectivity for all. An IT professional working on the North Pacific Regional Connectivity Investment Project in Palau (photo by Eric Sales).

Spotlight: Papua New Guinea

Papua New Guinea (PNG) has taken a range of steps to implement Agenda 2030. The National Planning and Monitoring Responsibility Act, 2016 established a development planning framework that incorporates the Sustainable Development Goals (SDGs). It has established a multitiered SDGs governance mechanism, including the National SDG Inter-Ministerial Committee, technical working groups, and an SDG secretariat. In addition to Vision 2050 and the Medium-Term Development Plan III (2018–2022), the country has also prepared the Development Cooperation Policy, 2018–2022 for development partners to align with national priorities in addition to developing sector approaches such as the National Food Security Policy, 2018–2027. PNG presented its first voluntary national review of SDG implementation progress in 2020. The SDG Core Team—part of the governance mechanism—is responsible for SDG monitoring using a range of data sources from the National Statistical Office, the private sector, development partners, civil society, and academia. The Department of National Planning and Monitoring is developing a national data center that aims to track all development indicators for development plans and the SDGs.

ADB has supported PNG since 1971 as is the country's largest multilateral development partner. Recent assistance has focused on developing transport infrastructure, promoting renewable energy, expanding access to finance, and improving health services. ADB's country partnership strategy for Papua New Guinea, 2021–2025 has three pathways: economic growth through improvements to infrastructure and bolstering the private sector; improving governance, financial management, and institutional strengthening to cope with fragility; and inclusivity and resilience for human development and climate and disaster risks.

To support connectivity, ADB is financing investments in roads, bridges, and aviation. In July 2017, ADB approved the Sustainable Highlands Highway Investment Program (SHHIP) with a project ceiling of $1.0 billion. The SHHIP program will rehabilitate and sustainably maintain 430 km of the highway, upgrade bridges, improve road safety, help establish logistics platforms and services for agricultural production, and support transport sector reforms.

Through the Highlands Region Road Improvement Investment program, ADB has provided $400 million for the construction and rehabilitation of over 347km of roads in the highlands core road network. ADB also committed $90 million for the Bridge Replacement for Improved Rural Access Project, which included cofinancing of $58 million from the European Investment Bank, to replace 33 single-lane bridges with permanent two-lane bridges along five national highways. ADB is also providing $480 million

through the Civil Aviation Development Investment Program to improve 21 airports that handle the bulk of PNG's domestic passenger and freight traffic.

To promote access to energy, ADB has funded the Town Electrification Investment Program, with only two tranches totaling $150 million. The ADB is also supporting the Port Moresby Power Grid Development Project, set to be completed in July 2022. Collectively these projects are helping to expand renewable energy supply through hydropower generation, distribution, and transmission. A complementary grant provided by the governments of Japan and New Zealand, is helping connect households to the new electricity services.

To strengthen Public Sector Management, In December 2020, ADB approved and disbursed $100 million under the State-Owned Enterprises Reform Program, Sub-Program 1, a policy-based loan that supports comprehensive reform of SOEs, with two further sub-programs planned for 2021 and 2022. To promote health and wellbeing, the Health Services Sector Development Program, which is strengthening health services through policy reforms and direct investments in health systems. Meanwhile, the Rural Primary Health Services Delivery Project, will construct up to 32 new rural health posts and train health workers in better primary health care.

ADB's investments help boost farmer incomes and improve rural livelihoods. PNG is a recipient of ADB's regional loan for the Agricultural Value Chain Development Project, which supports Olam International Limited and its subsidiaries to improve agricultural value chains and bring significant positive impacts to farmers and the agribusiness industry. The company is financing midstream coffee and sugar processing expansions and permanent working capital investments for smallholder farmer supply, which will promote sustainable agricultural value chains.

Developing the finance sector is also essential for PNG's socioeconomic development. The proposed Improving Financial Access and Entrepreneurship Development Project will develop the finance sector by improving access to financial services and building the entrepreneurship capacities of households and micro, small, and medium-sized enterprises. This is especially important for low-income and hard-to-reach communities. ADB is also providing regional technical assistance for Supporting Finance Sector and Private Sector Development in the Pacific to enable job creation, entrepreneurship, creativity, and innovation; and promote the formalization and growth of micro, small, and medium-sized enterprises.

PNG is investing in the SDGs, and ADB programs support this agenda.

Progress on Selected Indicators

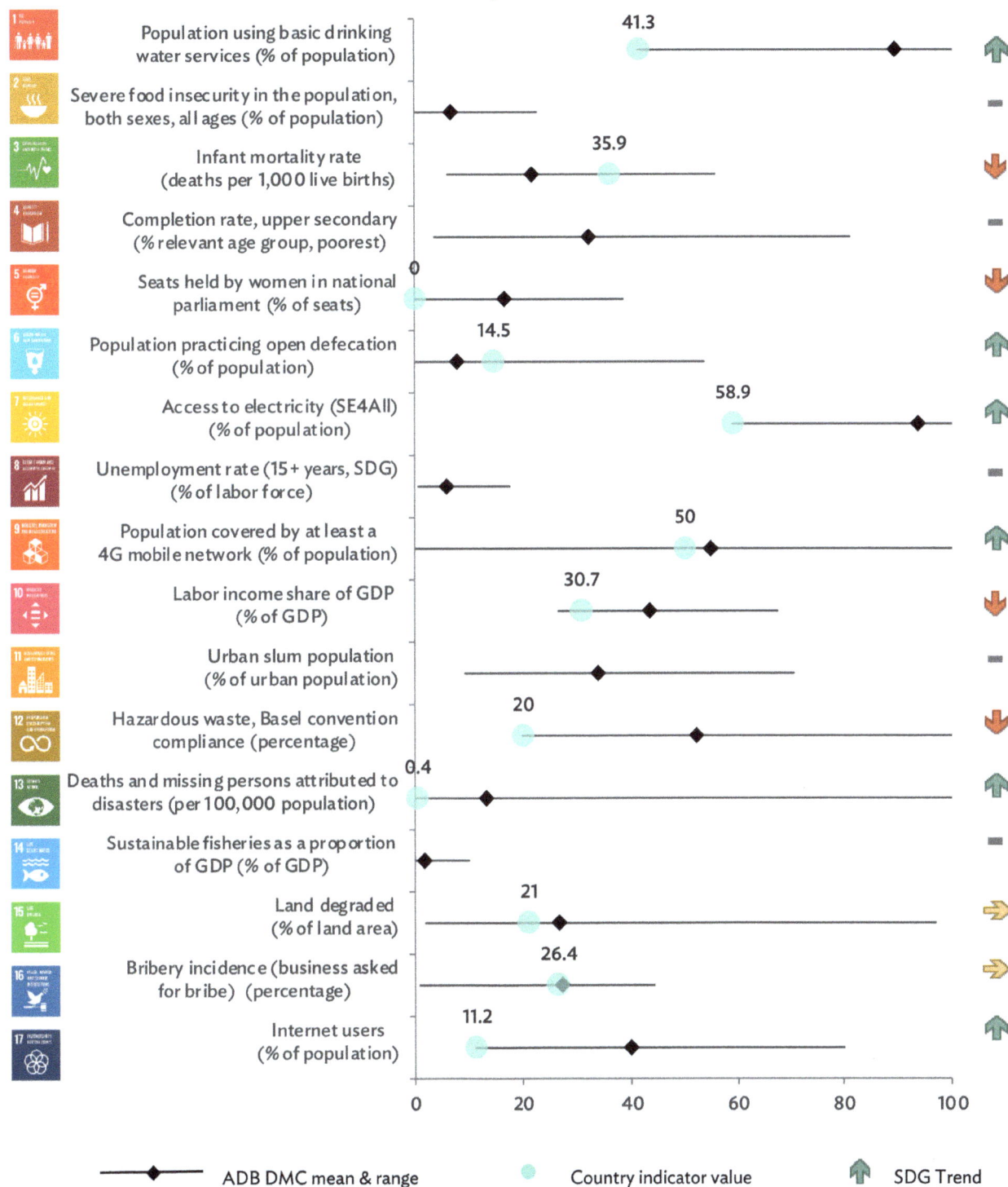

Indicator	Value
Population using basic drinking water services (% of population)	41.3
Severe food insecurity in the population, both sexes, all ages (% of population)	
Infant mortality rate (deaths per 1,000 live births)	35.9
Completion rate, upper secondary (% relevant age group, poorest)	
Seats held by women in national parliament (% of seats)	0
Population practicing open defecation (% of population)	14.5
Access to electricity (SE4All) (% of population)	58.9
Unemployment rate (15+ years, SDG) (% of labor force)	
Population covered by at least a 4G mobile network (% of population)	50
Labor income share of GDP (% of GDP)	30.7
Urban slum population (% of urban population)	
Hazardous waste, Basel convention compliance (percentage)	20
Deaths and missing persons attributed to disasters (per 100,000 population)	0.4
Sustainable fisheries as a proportion of GDP (% of GDP)	
Land degraded (% of land area)	21
Bribery incidence (business asked for bribe) (percentage)	26.4
Internet users (% of population)	11.2

Legend: ◆—— ADB DMC mean & range   ● Country indicator value   ⬆ SDG Trend

ADB = Asian Development Bank, DMC = developing member country, GDP = gross domestic product, SDG = Sustainable Development Goal, SE4All = sustainable energy for all.

Source: ADB analysis based on Asia-Pacific SDG Partnership. 2020. SDG Progress.

E. Finance and Knowledge Partnerships

The critical roles of finance, knowledge, capacity building support, and technology in realizing sustainable development aspirations are recognized in the SDG framework and the Addis Ababa Action Agenda on Financing for Development. There is broad recognition that public finance alone cannot meet the financing needs of the agenda, and that mobilizing finance from diverse sources, particularly the private sector, will be vital to achieve the SDGs. The fiscal and economic stresses caused by the COVID-19 pandemic have added to the challenge of raising the finance needed to achieve the SDGs. Alignment of private financing with the SDGs will therefore be essential.

These issues are also central to ADB's Strategy 2030, which positions ADB to become an ever more effective catalyzer of finance for development, provider of knowledge, convenor of partnerships, and promotes innovative integrated solutions (Figure 10). This section summarizes ADB's efforts to help countries mobilize finance for the SDGs, including by supporting private sector investment for the SDGs, and helping partner countries strengthen their SDG financing strategies and systems. It also reviews ADB's efforts to invest in knowledge directly related to SDG progress, attainment, and implementation. Partnerships are a crosscutting theme across these two issues.

Figure 12: ADB Mechanisms for Mobilizing the Additional Finance That the SDGs Require

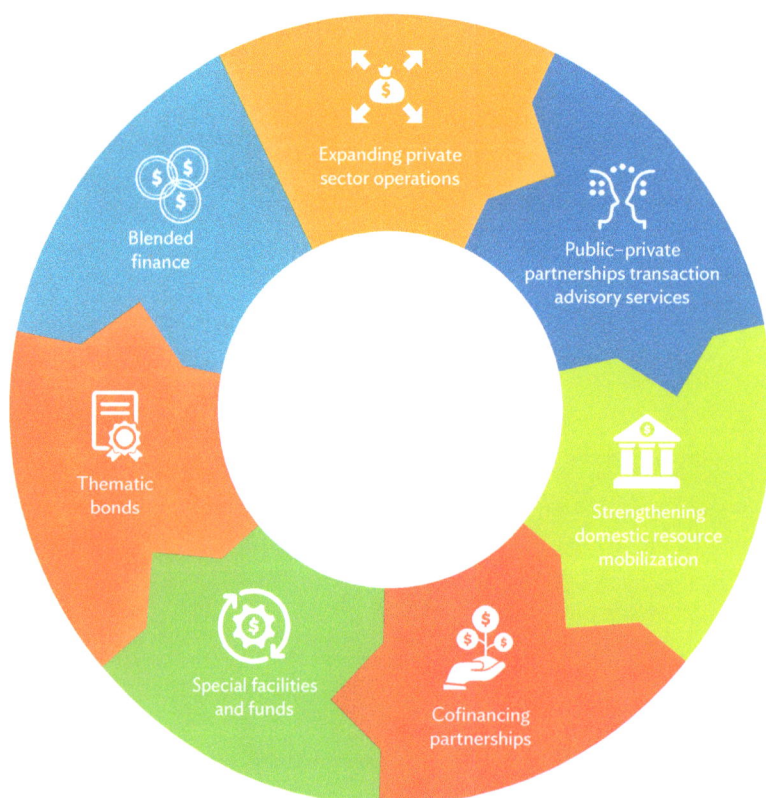

Source: Asian Development Bank.

1. Catalyzing and Mobilizing Financing

Expanding private sector operations. Strategy 2030 targets the continued expansion of ADB's private sector operations to reach one-third of its total operations in number by 2024, pursuing development impact as a key objective while ensuring profitability and commercial sustainability. ADB's Operational Plan for Private Sector Operations, 2019–2024 identifies SDG-aligned priority areas, as described in section I, and envisions more tailored debt and guarantee products, broader local currency offerings, and reinforced equity operations that meet the needs of clients in diverse markets (footnote 12). In 2020, ADB's Private Sector Operations Department launched ADB Ventures, an impact technology investment platform that aims to invest in young companies offering solutions that contribute to achieving the SDGs in Asia and the Pacific (Box 12).

Box 12: ADB Ventures

The ADB Ventures business model deploys venture capital investments and technical assistance to support early-stage technology businesses with fresh ideas that can have an impact on the Sustainable Development Goals (SDGs) in developing Asia and the Pacific. It aims to become the largest impact technology platform in the region, and crowd in more than $1 billion in risk capital to support the achievement of the SDGs in the region.

The inaugural ADB Ventures Investment Fund 1 has a 17-year fund life and is augmented by a 3-year, $12 million technical assistance program, allowing it to invest patient capital and help bring best-in-class technology to market. In April 2020, the fund raised $50 million from multilateral and bilateral development partners, exceeding its close target.[a]

Two technical assistance-funded activities—the ADB Ventures Seed Program and ADB Ventures Labs—will help ADB Ventures support young companies with fresh ideas. ADB Ventures Labs helps early-stage impact technology companies discover and develop opportunities to scale up in developing Asia and Pacific markets. The ADB Ventures Seed Program provides grants to help companies capitalize on market opportunities, and to derisk expansion into emerging markets that they might otherwise not enter.

Investment Fund 1 makes equity investments up to $4 million in impact technology companies, targeting commercial returns and focusing on clean technology, agricultural technology, financial technology, and health technology. The ADB Ventures Seed Program provides grant funding for rapid market validation.

ADB Ventures Labs has already helped more than 50 young impact technology companies explore opportunities in developing Asia. Initiatives include the Building Energy Challenge in partnership with New Energy Nexus, which matches the commercial real estate sector's demand for energy efficiency technologies with solutions such as energy management and smart building; and the Future Food Asia Awards 2020, teaming with ID Capital to identify agricultural technology and food security solutions for Asian Development Bank.

[a] The first investors in the fund are Finland's Ministry of Foreign Affairs, the Clean Technology Fund, the Nordic Development Fund, and the Republic of Korea's Ministry of Economy and Finance.

Source: ADB. 2020. At ADB Ventures the Bottom Line is to Help Developing Asia Meet the SDGs.

Public–private partnerships and transaction advisory services. Recognizing the crosscutting nature of the SDGs and the enormous investment needs, ADB supports public–private partnerships (PPPs) to help countries mobilize financial resources from diverse sources and ensure people have access to quality and affordable public services. Attracting private capital to infrastructure investments is often challenging because of a lack of well-prepared bankable projects. By helping develop, structure, and prepare bankable PPP projects, ADB aims to create more opportunities for private investment and reduce the costs of doing business, strengthen the quality of public service delivery, and promote private sector-led growth.

Blended finance. Blended finance has an important role to play in drawing in private capital.[30] ADB manages $709 million of concessional financing through eight blended finance funds and facilities. Since 2012, ADB has signed 18 transactions using a blended finance approach. These transactions have contributed to solving a range of financing challenges and delivered first-of-a-kind innovative financing solutions. These solutions have helped to derisk transactions and brought high-impact projects to market that would not have proceeded in the absence of concessional financing. These investments reflect the development finance institutions' agreed principles on the use of blended concessional finance for private sector projects.[31] They include additionality, crowding-in of private finance, commercial sustainability, reinforcing markets, and promoting high standards. ADB is also developing a private sector window under its concessional Asian Development Fund 13 cycle to support transactions in the region's poorest countries, including fragile and conflict-affected situations (FCAS) and small island developing states (SIDS).

Building cofinancing partnerships. Cofinancing partnerships are another focus of ADB efforts to catalyze and mobilize finance to achieve the SDGs. ADB seeks to build strong partnerships for resource mobilization across all its operations with private and public financial institutions and traditional and new development partners. Efforts are underway to engage diverse cofinancing partners, from the JP Morgan Chase Foundation to the New Development Bank, and enable their participation in ADB programs through streamlined processes. Strategy 2030 targets a substantial increase, with every $1.00 in financing for its private sector operations matched by $2.50 in long-term cofinancing by 2030.

Raising capital through thematic bonds. In addition, ADB has sought to support the development of thematic bonds since 2015 by issuing green, climate, and social bonds from its own balance sheet. By October 2020, green bond issuances exceed $7.7 billion and issuances for ADB's gender, health, and water bonds totaled $2.22 billion. ADB has also supported its clients in structuring bond issuances. For example, in 2016, ADB supported the Philippines' first climate bond issuance of $225 million equivalent, in conjunction with a loan of $37.7 million and a guarantee to the Tiwi–MakBan geothermal power facilities.

In 2018, ADB invested $155 million in climate bond issuances to finance B.Grimm Power Public Company Limited's solar plants in Thailand. The following year, ADB invested $20 million in AC Energy's first climate bond issuance, the proceeds of which will finance renewable energy projects in Indonesia, the Philippines, and Viet Nam. In March 2020, ADB approved a regional technical assistance program under the ASEAN Plus Three (ASEAN+3) Bond Markets Initiative to scale up the development of the local currency denominated thematic bond market in ASEAN+3.[32]

---

[30] Deployment of common blended finance strategies and tools, such as credit enhancement products and guarantees, can help draw in the private sector by improving risk–return profiles and mitigating risks.

[31] DFI Working Group on Blended Concessional Finance for Private Sector. 2017. Report prepared by a group of DFIs including ADB.

[32] ASEAN+3 consist of the 10 ASEAN members and Japan, the PRC, and the Republic of Korea.

Strengthening domestic financing for the Sustainable Development Goals. In addition to providing direct support to countries' efforts to finance the SDGs through its projects and associated financing, ADB helps countries mobilize finance to achieve their development aspirations and complements this assistance with knowledge and policy dialogue (Box 13). ADB is supporting countries such as Indonesia to develop and structure SDG-focused investment vehicles and funds. Helping countries enhance their domestic resource mobilization efforts is an important element of these strategies, and a vital element of recovery from the COVID-19 pandemic. Another way ADB seeks to enhance domestic resource mobilization is by supporting reforms in revenue collection, including tax systems and enforcement, through its operations and technical assistance. Tax yields in Asia and the Pacific have remained low despite strong and steady gross domestic product growth before the pandemic.

ADB technical assistance to strengthen DMCs' anti-money-laundering frameworks, including the transparency of beneficial ownership information, helps prevent illicit financial flows. ADB also supports its DMCs in meeting international tax integrity standards, including protecting themselves against aggressive forms of tax evasion, while enhancing capacity and regional cooperation among tax authorities. In collaboration with the Economic and Social Commission for Asia and the Pacific (ESCAP), the International Monetary Fund, and the Organisation for Economic Co-operation and Development (OECD), ADB has conducted capacity building programs on compliance risk management, base erosion and profit shifting practices, digitalization, and tax policy and statistics across 16 countries. ADB also produces regular comparative assessments of regional tax administration systems.

The multi-partner Domestic Resource Mobilization Trust Fund, established in July 2017, provides financing to complement and enable these measures. It has supported revenue modeling through value-added tax or tax incentive reform in Azerbaijan, the Lao PDR, and Solomon Islands, and a review of financial market tax policy in Armenia. In Cambodia, the Philippines, Thailand, and Viet Nam, the fund has supported property tax and land management reforms. The fund has also supported better tax compliance and risk management through strengthened systems and digitalization in Azerbaijan, Maldives, and the Philippines.

Box 13: Knowledge and Exchange on Financing for Development

The Asian Development Bank (ADB) has supported the Asia-Pacific Development Effectiveness Facility to develop tools and analysis to help developing member countries understand their options for financing their sustainable development strategies. The facility, for which the United Nations Development Programme (UNDP) serves as secretariat, has supported countries across the region, including the Lao People's Democratic Republic, Mongolia, Nepal, and the Philippines, to undertake development finance and aid assessments that quantify and analyze available sources of financing for their development plans. These analyses have highlighted the need to steer private sector and other sources of capital to support sustainable development.

Countries are leveraging this analytical work as they seek to develop integrated national financing frameworks to help realize their financing aspirations for the Sustainable Development Goals (SDGs) as part of the follow-up to the Addis Ababa Action Agenda. This national engagement informs ADB's partnership with UNDP to develop pilot SDG country implementation snapshots to complement ADB's country partnership strategies. ADB is also helping UNDP reform the Asia-Pacific Development Effectiveness Facility to focus on financing for the SDGs and reestablish itself as the Asia-Pacific SDG Financing Platform with a stronger emphasis on supporting government engagement with the private sector on these themes.

Source: Asian Development Bank.

Building on these ongoing efforts, ADB is establishing a regional hub on domestic resource mobilization and international tax cooperation. The hub will encourage close collaboration among the finance and tax authorities and practitioners of DMCs and other international organizations to enable knowledge sharing and strengthen cooperation on tax policy and tax administration across Asia and Pacific economies.

2. Fostering Knowledge, Policy Dialogue, and Capacity Building

ADB's engagement on the SDG agenda is complemented by knowledge and technical capacity building programs that focus on specific aspects of the SDGs and involve diverse partners. Supporting exchanges in experience among developing countries is an important feature of many of these efforts.

Participation in regional and global policy processes. ADB contributes to the Asia-Pacific Forum on Sustainable Development, an annual intergovernmental forum and regional platform for supporting countries in the implementation of Agenda 2030. The forum provides a regional input to the global High-Level Political Forum on Sustainable Development, convened by the UN Department for Economic and Social Affairs, where progress on the SDGs is reviewed each year, and where ADB convenes side events providing a regional perspective on SDG implementation. ADB has also hosted convenings during the UN General Assembly SDG Summit for senior government representatives, independent experts, and international organizations to support the SDG implementation snapshots initiative in Asia and the Pacific.

ADB's engagement with these processes is supported by the tripartite Asia-Pacific SDG Partnership established in September 2015 between ADB, ESCAP, and the United Nations Development Programme (UNDP) to provide knowledge and data on progress toward the SDGs. The partners produce the annual joint Asia-Pacific SDG Partnership report that provides a regional perspective on a theme relevant to Agenda 2030 implementation and the planned policy dialogue at the High-Level Political Forum (Box 14). The partnership also maintains the SDG Data portal, a compilation of data on official SDG indicators and related sources that allows analysis and assessment of regional progress toward the SDGs.

ADB also leverages its partnerships with UN agencies to provide inputs into related policy processes on financing for the SDGs, such as follow-ups to the Addis Ababa Action Agenda on financing for development.

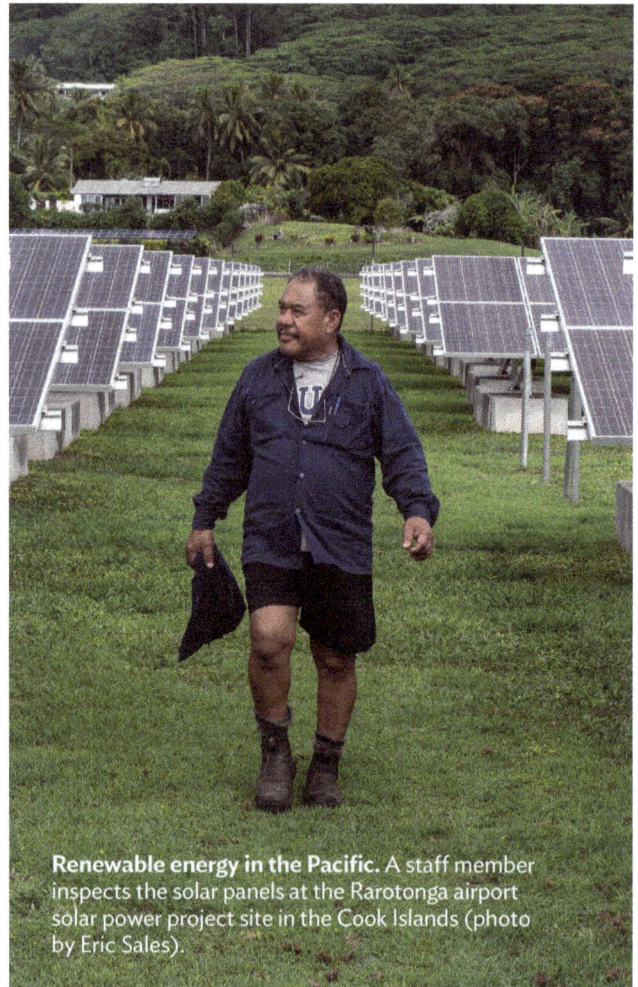

Renewable energy in the Pacific. A staff member inspects the solar panels at the Rarotonga airport solar power project site in the Cook Islands (photo by Eric Sales).

Support for environment-related goals in national planning. The environmental SDGs are critical to the sustainable development of the region, but progress on these goals has been slow and has often been underemphasized. In 2016, to strengthen DMCs' knowledge and capacity to integrate environment dimensions of the SDGs into national policy-making and planning processes, ADB developed regional technical assistance for Supporting Implementation of Environment-Related Sustainable Development Goals in Asia and the Pacific. Through a regional stocktaking review, challenges and opportunities were identified and a compendium of technical guidance for policy makers was disseminated and validated at a regional workshop. During 2018–2020, Mongolia, the Philippines, and Viet Nam received targeted support to improve policy coherence and integration of environmental considerations into broader development decisions.

Strengthening implementation in national and subnational contexts. ADB plays a role in strengthening national coordination mechanisms with other development actors including governments, international development partners, the private sector, and civil society. Examples include coleading sector coordination groups in Myanmar in sectors such as transport, where ADB has strong expertise. ADB also recognizes the importance of supporting localization of the SDGs, particularly in DMCs where governance is increasingly decentralized. ADB's regional knowledge and support technical assistance for Strengthening Institutions for Localizing Agenda 2030 for Sustainable Development works to raise awareness, build knowledge, and support innovative institutional capacity building to enable effective localization of the SDGs in DMCs, particularly in Cambodia, Indonesia, Mongolia, the PRC, and the Philippines. In 2020, the project supported an e-learning course on localization for DMCs and ADB staff. It has also supported a range of analysis and knowledge work related to SDG localization.

Measuring progress through better data. Recognizing the critical gaps in SDG data availability, ADB's Economic Research and Regional Cooperation Department supports technical assistance programs that seek to strengthen capacity, particularly within national statistics offices, to measure progress toward the SDGs in ADB DMCs. Since 2016, ADB's central statistical database, the Key Indicators database, and the annual publication, *Key Indicators for Asia and the Pacific*, have also included a focus on SDG progress. In 2019, ADB made its Key Indicators database available online, enabling easy access to SDG data within member economies and comparisons of SDG progress across countries. As many SDG indicators are survey-based, ADB has also assisted in the use of digital technology to conduct surveys more efficiently and in the use of satellite imagery to develop more granular and timely SDG data on poverty and agriculture. ADB also produced a study on the Readiness of National Statistical Systems in Asia and the Pacific for Leveraging Big Data to Monitor the SDGs, a knowledge product that highlights the need to harness big data ecosystems through partnerships, frameworks, and communication strategies.

Knowledge platforms. ADB has invested in diverse knowledge sharing platforms, many of which use the SDGs as a framework for stakeholder engagement. For example, ADB's Development Asia portal, launched in July 2017, provides short and accessible briefs on solutions to development challenges across the region that are cross-referenced to the SDGs. Regionally focused programs have also been developed. For example, ADB's Southeast Asia Development Solutions Knowledge and Innovation Platform (SEADS) supports knowledge exchange to help Southeast Asian countries become high-income, knowledge-driven, and sustainable economies. The Southeast Asia Development Symposium complements this platform by hosting exchanges on critical development issues, such as digital innovation.

ADB's Youth for Asia initiative has supported efforts to involve youth in the implementation of the SDGs, and partnered with Plan International to produce a knowledge product that shows how such engagement promotes progress toward the SDGs. ADB is also providing regional technical assistance on Building the Capacity of Journalists from Developing Member Countries in Asia and the Pacific to encourage high-quality journalism on economic and social development issues in Asia and the Pacific and achievement of the SDGs.

Strengthening results management. Supporting results management for the SDGs is an overarching priority for ADB. ADB collaborates with other MDBs, including as chair of the MDB Working Group on Managing for Development Results, to share its practices, learn from others' experiences, and advance common approaches to the SDGs. The working group provides a regular forum for the MDBs to share information on their institutional responses to the SDGs. The group undertook an initial stocktaking of approaches in 2018 and has since worked to advance common approaches to aligning results measurement and management with the SDGs. In December 2020, ADB and the Islamic Development Bank as chair of the Heads of MDBs group coordinated the first joint report to showcase the collective contributions of 11 MDBs and the International Monetary Fund to help countries achieve the 2030 Agenda for Sustainable Development. The MDBs also coordinate their engagement with related policy support partnerships such as the Global Partnership for Effective Development Co-operation.

In addition, as a member of the results community hosted by the OECD, ADB participates in OECD-facilitated reporting on its development finance, including through the Total Official Support for Sustainable Development initiative, which encourages reporting on the alignment of projects with the SDGs. ADB has participated in the multi-donor reference group guiding the development of the OECD Development Assistance Committee Guiding Principles for Managing for Sustainable Development Results. Since 2017, ADB has also worked with the African Development Bank, the Inter-American Development Bank, and the Korea Development Institute to jointly convene government stakeholders and leading experts each year to explore issues related to operationalizing the SDGs in national results management processes.

Technology and innovation. SDG 17 and ADB's Strategy 2030 highlight the importance of promoting innovative technologies as a driver for sustainable development. This is a core institutional priority that includes diverse initiatives including ADB's High-Level Technology Fund; internal incentives to promote and showcase innovation in ADB operations; and the Tech for Impact platform, which fosters interactive exchange on technology solutions to development challenges. ADB launched the <u>Digital Innovation Sandbox Program</u> in April 2019 to catalyze the infusion of new technologies to improve operations and accelerate sustainable development. The program supports innovative development solutions and the piloting of real-life scenarios to build capacity and overcome challenges. For example, the sandbox helped pilot a digital identity system in Papua New Guinea to promote financial inclusion. An Open Innovation Platform that includes institutional <u>partnerships with leading technology companies such as Microsoft</u> supports the initiative.

Standing strong. The Punakha dzong temple in Bhutan survived a massive flooding in 1994, when the two rivers surrounding the fortress overflowed due to rains (photo by Eric Sales).

Spotlight: Indonesia

The Sustainable Development Goals (SDGs) feature strongly in Indonesia's development architecture. The government has established multi-stakeholder mechanisms and a legal regulatory framework for SDG implementation, and integrated SDG targets and indicators into national and subnational development plans. SDG targets are well integrated into the National Medium-Term Development Plan, 2020–2024. Indonesia launched a road map for the SDGs for 2019–2030 in October 2019 and has developed innovative financing instruments to increase its SDG financing options such as *sukuk* (sharia compliant) and public–private blended finance platforms for infrastructure. Statistics Indonesia—the national statistical office—measures progress using its adapted SDG indicators list, sector data from line ministries, and the National Socioeconomic Survey. The government's new One Data Initiative aims to collate data across all national and subnational agencies on one platform.

The Asian Development Bank (ADB) country partnership strategy for Indonesia, 2020–2024 aligns with the country's national development plan, ADB's Strategy 2030, and the SDGs. It supports three strategic pathways: improving social well-being, accelerating economic recovery, and strengthening environmental resilience.

ADB provides a range of support for SDG implementation in Indonesia. Through the Fiscal and Public Expenditure Management Program, ADB has helped the government strengthen budget preparation, transparency, and monitoring; and implement reforms to improve the quality of government spending on health, education, social protection, and infrastructure. The program also helped align the government's medium-term expenditure with the National Medium-Term Development Plan, 2015–2019 and operationalize the national SDG implementation architecture. ADB has supported the process of linking these plans with the SDGs and developing the Indonesia SDG Roadmap.

PT Sarana Multi Infrastruktur (Persero), Indonesia's state-owned infrastructure finance company, has launched SDG Indonesia One, a dedicated financing platform that combines public and private funds to be channeled into infrastructure projects with focus on the SDGs. ADB has provided technical advice to this initiative. Targets to monitor overall achievements are linked to the SDGs.

ADB has also worked with SDG centers established at Indonesia's regional universities to support knowledge exchange on SDG implementation issues. For example, ADB worked with local government and other stakeholders in East Java to create dashboards to make easy-to-understand development data on child marriage available. The insights from the program are being used to support policy dialogue in the country on this vital but sensitive issue. ADB and the United Nations Development Programme jointly prepared an SDG Country Implementation Snapshot for Indonesia in 2020 to take stock of SDG implementation since 2015.

ADB has played a major role in financing climate-related projects in Indonesia, including by supporting greater use of renewable and efficient energy technologies. The Geothermal Power Generation Project will expand PT Geo Dipa Energi's geothermal power generation capacity and provide environmentally friendly base-load electricity to the Java–Bali electricity grid, avoiding emissions equivalent to more than 700,000 tons of carbon dioxide per year. ADB is also helping to expand electricity access and promote renewable energy in remote communities in eastern Indonesia through the Sustainable Energy Access in Eastern Indonesia–Electricity Grid Development Program. This results-based loan to PT Perusahaan Listrik Negara will contribute to the government's plans to increase the share of renewable energy in the total energy mix to 23% by 2025.

ADB has supported institutional arrangements for SDG implementation in Indonesia, and innovative approaches to financing SDG implementation.

Progress on Selected Indicators

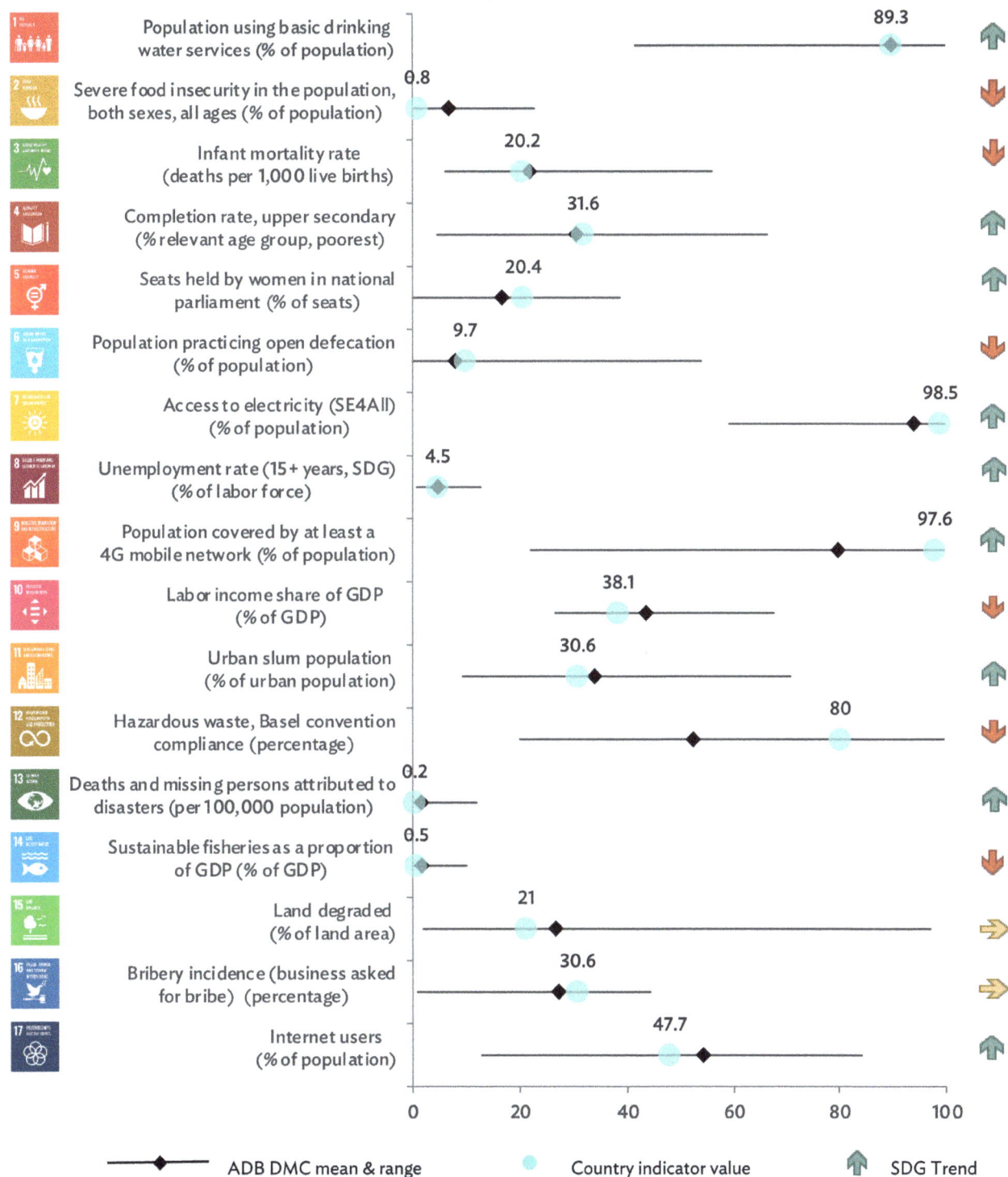

SDG	Indicator	Value	Trend
1	Population using basic drinking water services (% of population)	89.3	⬆
2	Severe food insecurity in the population, both sexes, all ages (% of population)	0.8	⬇
3	Infant mortality rate (deaths per 1,000 live births)	20.2	⬇
4	Completion rate, upper secondary (% relevant age group, poorest)	31.6	⬆
5	Seats held by women in national parliament (% of seats)	20.4	⬆
6	Population practicing open defecation (% of population)	9.7	⬇
7	Access to electricity (SE4All) (% of population)	98.5	⬆
8	Unemployment rate (15+ years, SDG) (% of labor force)	4.5	⬆
9	Population covered by at least a 4G mobile network (% of population)	97.6	⬆
10	Labor income share of GDP (% of GDP)	38.1	⬇
11	Urban slum population (% of urban population)	30.6	⬆
12	Hazardous waste, Basel convention compliance (percentage)	80	⬇
13	Deaths and missing persons attributed to disasters (per 100,000 population)	0.2	⬆
14	Sustainable fisheries as a proportion of GDP (% of GDP)	0.5	⬇
15	Land degraded (% of land area)	21	➡
16	Bribery incidence (business asked for bribe) (percentage)	30.6	➡
17	Internet users (% of population)	47.7	⬆

◆— ADB DMC mean & range   ● Country indicator value   ⬆ SDG Trend

ADB = Asian Development Bank, DMC = developing member country, GDP = gross domestic product, SDG = Sustainable Development Goal, SE4All = sustainable energy for all.

Source: ADB analysis based on Asia-Pacific SDG Partnership. 2020. SDG Progress.

III. Reinforcing ADB's Contributions to the Sustainable Development Goals at a Critical Juncture

Countries in Asia and the Pacific were off track to achieve the SDGs even before COVID-19 disrupted the lives of their people and economies in 2020. Many of the most devastating effects of the pandemic are linked in part to gaps in SDG attainment. ADB has responded swiftly and comprehensively to counter the severe macroeconomic and health impacts caused by COVID-19, developing a $20 billion response package and establishing a the COVID-19 Pandemic Response Option under ADB's Countercyclical Support Facility to help countries weather the macroeconomic and fiscal effects of the disease. Amid the crisis, the SDGs are more relevant than ever before, and provide a resonant agreed framework for recovery. Through Strategy 2030, ADB has committed to supporting its DMCs' efforts to achieve the SDGs, as described in this first ADB corporate report on ADB's response to the SDGs.

Embedding the Sustainable Development Goals in ADB systems. The SDGs are increasingly reflected in key institutional policies and processes, as set out in section I of this report. All ADB projects and programs are linked to the SDGs, and the corporate results framework (CRF) is aligned with SDG goals and targets. Key plans and programming templates increasingly include references to the SDGs. This is an iterative effort, and ADB continues to refine and improve its systems to align its programs with the SDGs and report on its support for this agenda, building on lessons learned and demands from its stakeholders. In 2021, ADB will further strengthen the SDG links in its project classification system, country partnership strategy (CPS) template and associated results framework, and project design and monitoring framework. ADB will continue to engage with other partners, including other MDBs and the OECD, on these efforts.

Deepening country and regional engagement on the 2030 Agenda. Ultimately, it is countries that have signed on to the SDGs and must take responsibility for their implementation. ADB has made significant efforts to engage with and support national SDG implementation efforts, as highlighted in the examples presented in section II of this report. While country programming reflects national needs and priorities, there are opportunities to deepen express alignment of this CPS process with identified SDG priorities. Continued support for localization of the SDGs, including through engagement at the subnational level, will be an important element.

Knowledge, learning, and reflection. ADB will continue to invest in knowledge that helps countries and stakeholders understand key issues related to SDG implementation and seize opportunities to make progress on this vital integrated agenda. Strengthening internal exchange and fostering dialogue on lessons learned through operations that seek to address the SDGs will also be a growing priority.

Deepening and sustaining innovative partnerships for the goals. ADB will continue to sustain and deepen ongoing partnerships for the SDGs, building on the strong foundations that have been established. ADB will continue to invest in its partnerships with UN agencies, and explore new partnerships with private sector actors and philanthropic organizations, including to support efforts to align financing with the SDGs.

Supporting recovery from the pandemic and accelerating progress. At this critical juncture, there is a need to analyze and assess the implications of the pandemic for SDG attainment, and ensure that COVID-19 recovery frameworks support countries to put themselves on a better path to achieve these ambitious goals. In this context, continued efforts to identify investments that can accelerate progress toward the SDGs in line with Strategy 2030 are needed, drawing on lessons from ongoing and completed ADB operations and wider analysis of development trends in the region. ADB will work to ensure its engagement and investment approaches help countries seize the opportunity to build back better from the pandemic and will develop tools and guidance for operations to achieve this goal. Support for domestic resource mobilization for the SDGs, and investments in quality infrastructure that promotes green, resilient, inclusive, and sustainable development will be vital.

As Asia and the Pacific continues its development journey and recovers from the COVID-19 pandemic, it is more important than ever to focus on the SDGs. ADB will remain a committed partner in this effort.

Figure 13: Evolution of ADB's Approach to the Sustainable Development Goals

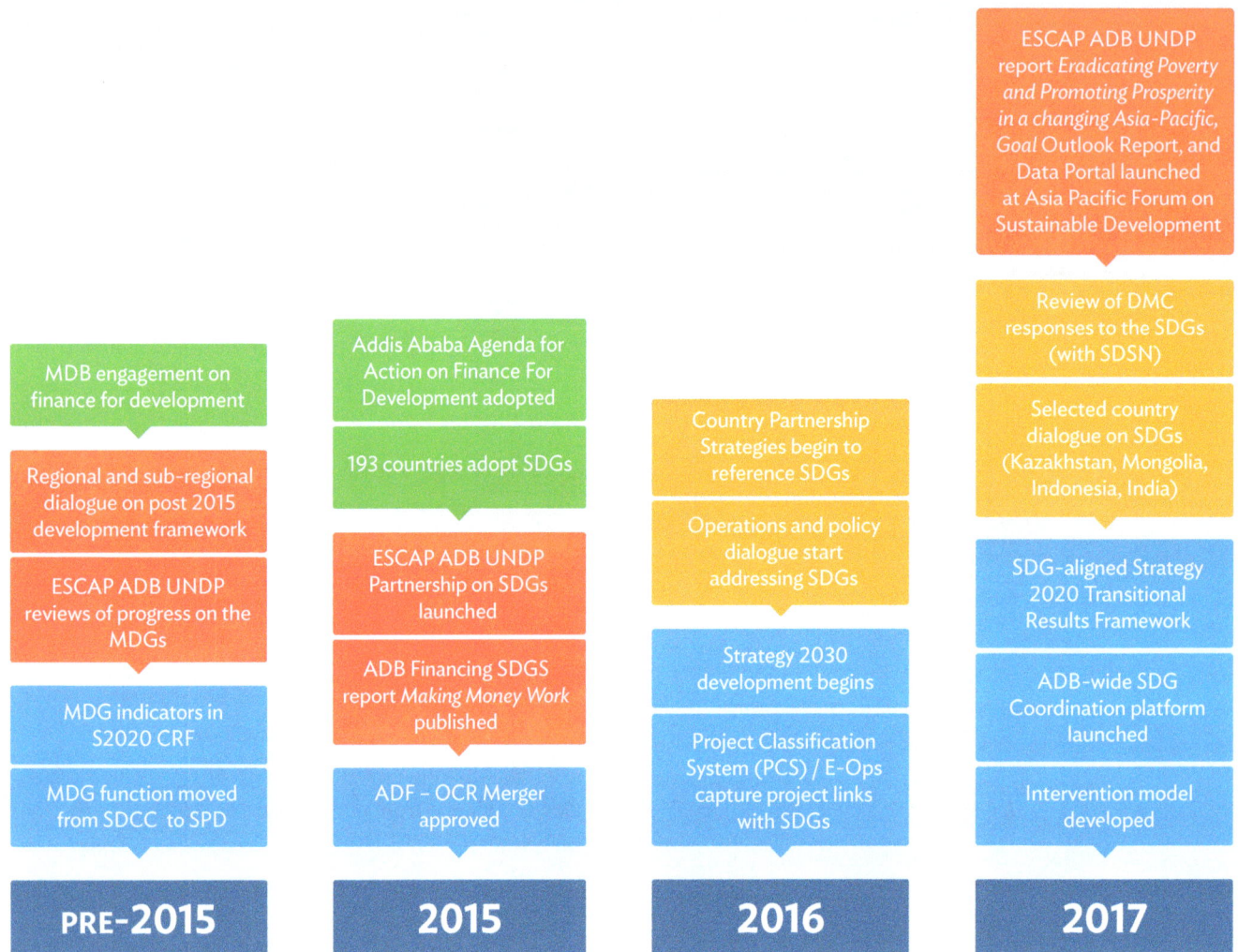

PRE-2015
- MDB engagement on finance for development
- Regional and sub-regional dialogue on post 2015 development framework
- ESCAP ADB UNDP reviews of progress on the MDGs
- MDG indicators in S2020 CRF
- MDG function moved from SDCC to SPD

2015
- Addis Ababa Agenda for Action on Finance For Development adopted
- 193 countries adopt SDGs
- ESCAP ADB UNDP Partnership on SDGs launched
- ADB Financing SDGS report *Making Money Work* published
- ADF – OCR Merger approved

2016
- Country Partnership Strategies begin to reference SDGs
- Operations and policy dialogue start addressing SDGs
- Strategy 2030 development begins
- Project Classification System (PCS) / E-Ops capture project links with SDGs

2017
- ESCAP ADB UNDP report *Eradicating Poverty and Promoting Prosperity in a changing Asia-Pacific, Goal* Outlook Report, and Data Portal launched at Asia Pacific Forum on Sustainable Development
- Review of DMC responses to the SDGs (with SDSN)
- Selected country dialogue on SDGs (Kazakhstan, Mongolia, Indonesia, India)
- SDG-aligned Strategy 2020 Transitional Results Framework
- ADB-wide SDG Coordination platform launched
- Intervention model developed

ADB = Asian Development Bank; ADF = Asian Development Fund; APFSD = Asia-Pacific Forum on Sustainable Development; CPS = country partnership strategy; CRF = corporate results framework; DEfR= Development Effectiveness Review; DMC = developing member country; E-Ops = E-Operations; ESCAP = Economic and Social Council for Asia and the Pacific; HLPF = High-Level Political Forum; MDB = multilateral development bank; MDG = Millennium Development Goal; MfDR = managing for development results; OCR = ordinary capital resources; PCS = project classification system; S2020 = Strategy 2020; S2030 = Strategy 2030; SDCC = Sustainable Development and Climate Change Department; SDG = Sustainable Development Goal; SDSN = Sustainable Development Solutions Network; SPD = Strategy, Policy and Review Department; THK = Tri Hita Karana; UNDP = United Nations Development Programme; UNGA = United Nations General Assembly; WG = working group.
Source: Asian Development Bank.

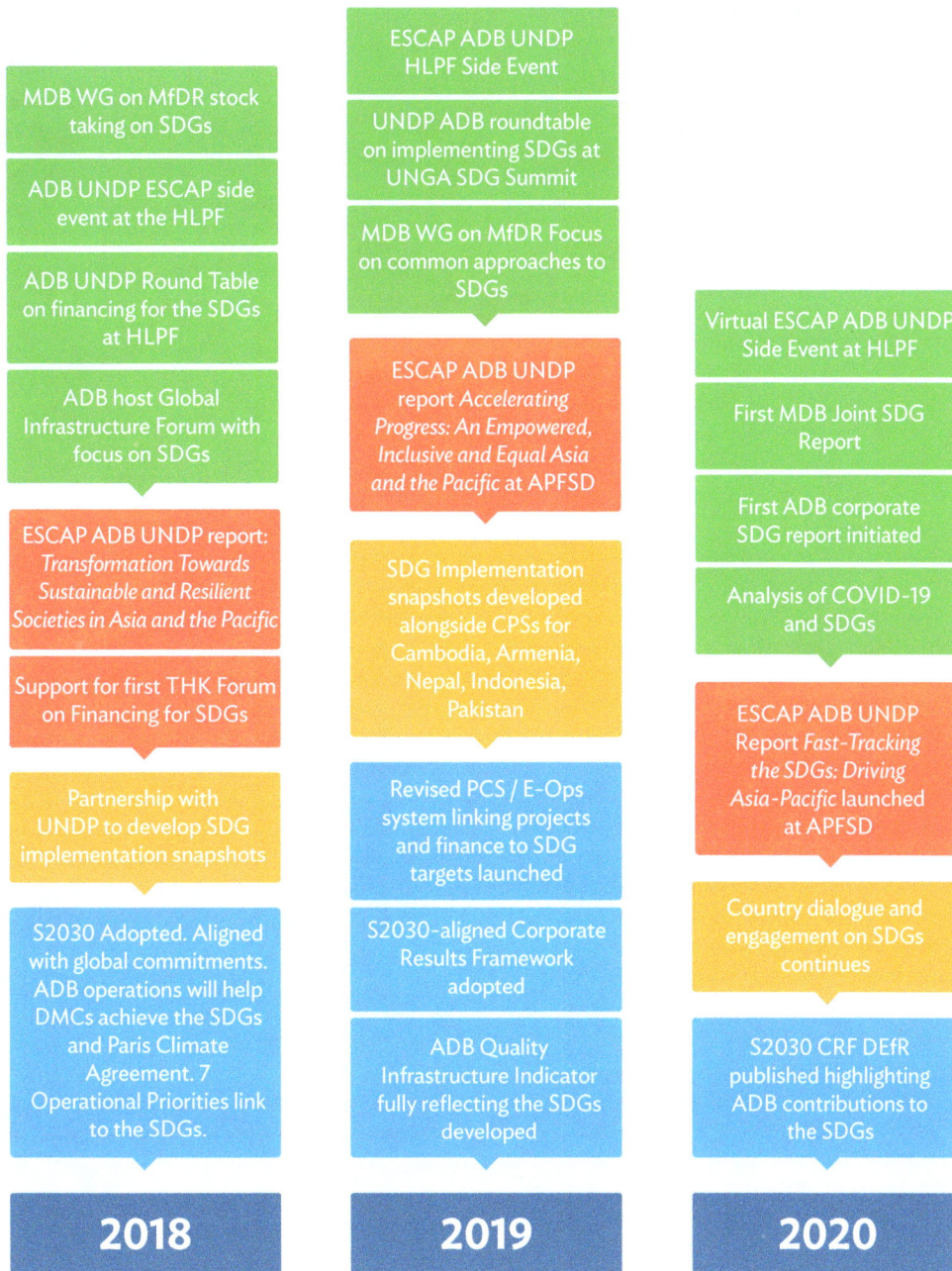

2018

- MDB WG on MfDR stock taking on SDGs
- ADB UNDP ESCAP side event at the HLPF
- ADB UNDP Round Table on financing for the SDGs at HLPF
- ADB host Global Infrastructure Forum with focus on SDGs
- ESCAP ADB UNDP report: *Transformation Towards Sustainable and Resilient Societies in Asia and the Pacific*
- Support for first THK Forum on Financing for SDGs
- Partnership with UNDP to develop SDG implementation snapshots
- S2030 Adopted. Aligned with global commitments. ADB operations will help DMCs achieve the SDGs and Paris Climate Agreement. 7 Operational Priorities link to the SDGs.

2019

- ESCAP ADB UNDP HLPF Side Event
- UNDP ADB roundtable on implementing SDGs at UNGA SDG Summit
- MDB WG on MfDR Focus on common approaches to SDGs
- ESCAP ADB UNDP report *Accelerating Progress: An Empowered, Inclusive and Equal Asia and the Pacific* at APFSD
- SDG Implementation snapshots developed alongside CPSs for Cambodia, Armenia, Nepal, Indonesia, Pakistan
- Revised PCS / E-Ops system linking projects and finance to SDG targets launched
- S2030-aligned Corporate Results Framework adopted
- ADB Quality Infrastructure Indicator fully reflecting the SDGs developed

2020

- Virtual ESCAP ADB UNDP Side Event at HLPF
- First MDB Joint SDG Report
- First ADB corporate SDG report initiated
- Analysis of COVID-19 and SDGs
- ESCAP ADB UNDP Report *Fast-Tracking the SDGs: Driving Asia-Pacific* launched at APFSD
- Country dialogue and engagement on SDGs continues
- S2030 CRF DEfR published highlighting ADB contributions to the SDGs

TIMELINE

- Internal Alignment
- Country
- Regional
- Global

With a little help from big sister. Saima, an 8-year-old student, helps out with her younger sibling's schoolwork (photo by Sara Farid).

Contributors

This report was overseen by Tomoyuki Kimura, director general, Strategy Policy and Partnerships Department (SPD) and Bernard Woods, Director of the Aid Effectiveness and Results Management Division. It was led by Smita Nakhooda, senior results management specialist SPD, and a core team including Mercedes Martin, Hazel Lalas and Frank Thomas. Focal points from across ADB provided invaluable inputs and review comments. Dave Pipon and Ma. Cecilia Landicho provided coordination support. Caroline Ahmad edited the report. Karmen Karamanian led design, in collaboration with Charlene Laxamana.

www.ingramcontent.com/pod-product-compliance
Lightning Source LLC
Chambersburg PA
CBHW050049220326
41599CB00045B/7346